CHOSEN FOR
GREATNESS

HOW ADOPTION CHANGES THE WORLD

PAUL J. BATURA

WITH A FOREWORD BY **ERIC METAXAS** AND
AN AFTERWORD BY **LARRY KING**

REGNERY
FAITH

Regnery Faith™ is a trademark of Salem Communications Holding Corporation; Regnery® is a registered trademark of Salem Communications Holding Corporation

Cataloging-in-Publication data on file with the Library of Congress

ISBN 978-1-62157-585-6

Published in the United States by
Regnery Faith
An imprint of Regnery Publishing
A Division of Salem Media Group
300 New Jersey Ave NW
Washington, DC 20001
www.RegneryFaith.com

Manufactured in the United States of America

10 9 8 7 6 5 4 3 2 1

Books are available in quantity for promotional or premium use. For information on discounts and terms, please visit our website: www.Regnery.com.

Distributed to the trade by
Perseus Distribution
250 West 57th Street
New York, NY 10107

For photo rights information, please see page 253.

To Riley (Julianna), Will (Joli), and Alex (Jennifer).

You didn't just change the world—you changed ours.

Thank you for giving your mom and me the privilege of

being your parents.

CONTENTS

God moves in mysterious ways; His wonders to perform;
He plans His footsteps in the sea, and rides upon the storm.
                                        —William Cowper (1731–1800)

People don't rise from nothing. We do owe something to parentage and patronage. The people who stand before kings may look like they did it all themselves. But in fact they are invariably the beneficiaries of hidden advantage and extraordinary opportunities and cultural legacies that allow them to learn and work hard and make sense of the world in ways others cannot. It makes a difference where and when we grew up. The culture we belong to and the legacies passed down by our forebears shape the patterns of our achievement in ways we cannot begin to imagine. It's not enough to ask what successful people are like, in other words. It is only by asking where they are from that we can unravel the logic behind who succeeds and who doesn't.[1]

                                        —Malcolm Gladwell

You go nowhere by accident.
Wherever you go,
God is sending you.
Wherever you are,
God has put you there.
God has a purpose
in your being there.
Christ lives in you
and has something
he wants to do
through you where you are.
Believe this and go in the
grace and love and
power of Jesus Christ.[2]

—Rev. Richard Halverson

The Gospel is not a picture of adoption, adoption is a picture of the Gospel.[3]

—John Piper

FOREWORD

When I set out to write my book *Seven Men: And the Secret of Their Greatness*, I did so with a simple but significant goal.

At the time, I knew there was a crisis of manhood in America. And along with that crisis—and in a way the cause of it too—I saw a four-decade-long reluctance to embrace and celebrate heroes, and I wanted to do something about it.

Seven Men, and later, *Seven Women*, were my attempts to shine a spotlight on some of the most heroic people who have ever lived. People like the late Olympian Eric Liddell, Joan of Arc, Corrie ten Boom, baseball and Civil Rights icon Jackie Robinson, and Mother Teresa.

In compiling these profiles, I was reminded of what President Reagan said in his first inaugural address. Speaking from the porch of the sunsplashed Capitol building on that cold January day in 1981, our nation's fortieth president declared, "Those who say that we're in a time when there are no heroes. They just don't know where to look."

I strongly agree.

Why I chose the people I did was of course subjective, but everyone I selected shared a single, particular trait, and it's the secret to their greatness. All of the people I wrote about were somehow self-sacrificing, which is to say they used what they had been given by God to bless others. In doing so, they were expressing unconditional love for their fellow man, which is what the New Testament calls *agape*, a love of and from God.

And *agape* love—love that gives without any expectation of something in return—is the type of love that sits at the center of the pro-life movement. It's this type of love that drives so many of the sacrificial souls who serve the women and children most in need.

I know this because I'm married to one of these wonderful people. My wife, Susanne, has for over ten years been the director of Avail, a pregnancy center right here in Manhattan, where we live. She doesn't do it for the money. Trust me. She does it because she wants to help the women who have been told they don't have any real choice but to end the lives of the babies inside them. She wants to help them choose to bring those babies into the world, and in so doing she wants to help the whole world see the most empowering, significant, and beautiful thing any human can ever do—to help someone else, especially those who are powerless.

I share that same conviction and goal.

It was a similar conviction and heart for both the most vulnerable among us—and a desire to highlight the good among us—that led my friend, Paul Batura of Focus on the Family, to write this book. As an adoptive father of three boys himself, Paul wanted to tell the stories rarely told surrounding some of our world's most well-known adoptees and foster-care children.

His effort has resulted in a captivating and compelling page-turner. How I wish I could give you a copy! But since you already have this one, I'm glad I don't need to.

But seriously, folks, I'm not the kind of person who believes in coincidences—because I believe in a sovereign God who watches over the affairs of women and men. As such, no adoption is an accident. In fact, every adoption was planned long ago, a fact that makes these stories all the more remarkable. Indeed, as you'll see, behind every adoption is a series of intimate, dramatic, and God-ordained moments.

As a writer and broadcaster, I've made a career analyzing the way the world has changed and is changing; and I've interviewed many of the people responsible. From that experience and those conversations, I can attest to the fact adoption is changing the world we live in for the better. And as I discovered in my own "Seven" series, all of these adoptees have done something great, not because *they* were great, but because the people surrounding them were willing to sacrifice on their behalf.

I have no doubt these stories will bless you. So leap in and get blessed. I'll just get out of the way now...

Eric Metaxas
New York City
September 2016

ON THE VERGE OF EVERYTHING

E ver since I was a young boy, especially while sitting or walking along the South Shore sands of Long Island with my mother, I loved to ask questions. I especially liked to ask "What if?" questions about people. As I grew older, the questions became more informed and often revolved around our mutual love of history.

For example: What if Christopher Columbus had never sailed from Spain? What if the late summer fog of 1776 had quickly lifted over Brooklyn and George Washington and his troops were captured by the British? What if the Confederacy prevailed against the Union Army? What if President Kennedy survived the assassin's bullet—or President Reagan had not?

There's no way my immature mind could have realized it, but at the core of my "What if?" questions was an ageless and fundamental curiosity. Do our choices in life really matter—or is God behind the curtain pulling all the strings?

Or put more bluntly: Is it God or is it man who is in the middle of all things?

Or could it be that yes, God is in charge, but as His servants, our actions do matter and have consequences? After all, it was Solomon who declared that "All the days planned for me were written in your book before I was one day old" (Psalms 139:16).

Scientists and theologians call this an "antinomy"—an apparent contradiction. How could it be that God is sovereign and yet man still has free will to make decisions that matter?

What the secularists have called "fate"—the belief that things randomly come to be—people of faith have called "Providence" or "destiny"—a belief that a supernatural intercessor is overseeing life on earth. For example, reflecting on the miraculous birth of America in 1776, it was Virginia statesman John Page who wrote to Thomas Jefferson saying, "We know the race is not to the swift nor the battle to the strong. Do you not think an angel rides in the whirlwind and directs this storm?"[1]

PROVIDENCE AND ADOPTION

Since receiving the privilege of adopting our three sons, my wife, Julie, and I have allowed ourselves to ponder the "What ifs?" surrounding their lives and adoptions. What if their birth mothers had not chosen to courageously carry them to term? What if they had chosen someone else to adopt them? What if they had decided not to make an adoption plan at all?

All of these questions, some admittedly haunting ones at that, led me to start pondering the "What ifs?" of other well-known adoptees. For example, what if John Hancock had become a pastor instead of a politician? What if Nelson Mandela's adoptive father didn't have deft leadership skills that rubbed off on his son? What if Steve Jobs had been adopted by a couple in Florida instead of one in Silicon Valley?

Whenever I would look up their stories and try to learn more about the circumstances surrounding their respective adoptions, most of the information was limited to a single sentence or perhaps just a paragraph or two.

But there had to be more. How could such an emotional, monumental, and transformational moment be reduced to a passing reference?

Was their adoption a mere factual footnote in their lives, like their birth date or hometown, or was it one of the driving forces behind the stories of their successes?

In the following pages, I believe you'll see that every single one of the individuals profiled didn't succeed *in spite of* being adopted or intimately cared for by someone other than their biological parent; they rose to their level of accomplishment in no small part *because of* their adoption and relationship with their new parent or parents.

In fact, their adoption didn't just change the course of their lives and the families who embraced and loved them. Instead, you'll see their adoption has changed—and is changing—the course of your life and mine.

You'll also see, I hope, that adoption, like life itself, is a gritty and an often imperfect process. It's nothing like you see in the movies, watch on television, or even read in a bestselling novel.

Indeed, it's far more dramatic—because the stories you're about to read are true and involve real people who made and are making a significant difference in the world.

Each and every person featured in the following pages was chosen for greatness.

In the end, you'll be reminded that *every* adoption puts *every* child on the verge of *everything* because, in the words of Henry David Thoreau, "*Every* child begins the world again."[2]

CHAPTER ONE

STEVE JOBS

In the early light of October 5, 2011, at his home in Palo Alto, California, Apple co-founder Steve Jobs quietly studied the faces of the loved ones surrounding his bed. He was fading in and out of consciousness. Closest to him was his wife of twenty years, Laurene. She was monitoring the pace and frequency of his breathing. He seemed to be climbing, as if ascending a steep mountain trail. Their three children, Reed, Erin, and Eve, ringed the perimeter of the room keeping vigil. Steve's sisters, Patty Jobs and Mona Simpson, were also present.

The intensely private entrepreneurial tech giant who had once declared his goal "to change the world" was at the end of a long and painful illness. Originally diagnosed with pancreatic cancer in 2004, Jobs suffered and bravely managed a myriad of health-related complications over the course of seven years. He took three official leaves of absence, including one for a liver transplant in 2009, before resigning as CEO in August of 2011. Investors and admirers tracked and followed his every move. Paparazzi camped outside his home and in the bushes of medical office parking lots, hoping to catch a snapshot of the ailing Silicon Valley titan.

But as summer turned to fall, it became clear Steve Jobs was dying. There would be no more treatments or experimental medications. He was homebound, too frail and weak to venture outside the British Country style house on Waverley Street. Knowing the curtain was falling, a small number of Apple executives, all from his inner circle, many of whom were Christian, began making regular trips to the Jobs' residence. Naturally, business was always discussed during these meetings. According to those present, Steve would light up whenever a new project or company challenge was put forth for debate. But those closest to the Apple guru, speaking on condition of anonymity, would later say that during these final visits, Steve was more interested in talking about religion and the afterlife than software and technology. He was unsettled. He had questions. Big ones. Questions such as, "What really happens when we die?"; "Where do we go?"; or "What's it like *there*?" became popular topics of conversation.

Although Jobs spent his early years attending a local Lutheran church with his parents and sister, he grew frustrated as a teenager with traditional Christianity. Specifically, he struggled with the seeming contradiction of how an all-loving God could allow the suffering and starvation of innocent people, especially children. The standard answers from his pastor and parents no longer satisfied him.

"The juice goes out of Christianity," he told his biographer, Walter Isaacson, "when it becomes too based on faith rather than on living like Jesus or seeing the world as Jesus sees it."[1] And so, as a young man, Jobs began exploring and embracing the world of Zen Buddhism. He intently studied its tenets. Shortly after dropping out of Reed College in Oregon, Jobs even traveled to India where he considered joining a Zen monastery. He regularly meditated and voraciously read religious texts. He said he wanted to experience spiritual highs, not engage in dry doctrinal debates of Christianity. Returning three years later with a shaved head and wearing traditional Indian garb, he began practicing a modified version of the ancient faith. In the office, Jobs would often wear jeans without shoes. According to Steve, Buddhism seemed to complement his work ethic and worldview. He appreciated its simplicity. But now he was at the end of his life. And the specificity, urgency, and poignancy of his questions hinted Steve Jobs was still searching for what he had never seen or experienced since childhood: peace and assurance.

BEGINNINGS

Steve Paul Jobs was born in San Francisco on February 24, 1955, to Joanne Carole Schieble, a University of Wisconsin graduate student. Miss Schieble and Steve's biological father, Abdulfattah "John" Jandali, met at the university where Jandali was pursuing a Ph.D. in political science and served as Joanne's teaching assistant. Coming from a German Catholic farming family, Schieble's parents weren't supportive of the young couple's relationship. According to press reports, Joanne's father threatened to withhold ongoing financial assistance if their daughter didn't break up with the Muslim graduate student. Miss Schieble's father was dying, and she didn't want to upset the family. Furthermore, the young twenty-two-year-old decided neither she nor Jandali had the financial means to raise a baby.

And so, Joanne Schieble decided to make an adoption plan for her unborn son.

In early 1955, just months before she was expected to give birth, Joanne Schieble left Wisconsin and moved to San Francisco to be cared for by an obstetrician who quietly ministered to unwed mothers. This doctor would deliver the baby and then work with the birth mother to find suitable adoptive parents. At the time, as was customary, all the adoptions arranged by the doctor were "closed"—meaning neither party knew or would ever know one another. In selecting an adoptive family, Joanne had one main requirement. She wanted the family to be college-educated. A couple was quickly identified. They were Catholic, the husband was a lawyer, and the family was wealthy. However, the couple changed their mind after Steve was born. They wanted a girl. It was time to find a new adoptive couple—and quickly.

A DREAM COME TRUE

Paul and Clara Jobs were married in 1946, shortly after Paul was discharged from the Coast Guard after serving in World War II. Clara was previously married, but widowed after her first husband was killed in action during the war. Paul was an engine mechanic who loved to tinker with cars. Clara worked as a bookkeeper.

They didn't have a lot of money, but they were in love and they were happy. Mutually supportive of one another, they longed to welcome a baby into their home. An ectopic pregnancy came as a crushing blow to the young couple, and for nine long years they tried unsuccessfully to start a family. Finally, they were referred to the aforementioned Bay Area doctor who was caring for unwed mothers. They declared their desire to adopt. Whether a girl or a boy didn't matter to them.

At first glance, Paul and Clara Jobs were a poor match for Joanne Schieble's baby boy. Besides lacking the one main requirement of a college education, Paul's life was lacking any notable accomplishment. Having run into minor trouble during his military tenure, he never rose above the lowest rank of Seaman. After marrying, the six-foot-tall tattooed mechanic, short on money, moved himself and his wife back to Wisconsin to live with Clara's parents. After several years they relocated to Indiana where Paul worked a blue-collar job as a machinist for International Harvester. He later quit and began selling used cars. Clara loved San Francisco, though, and convinced her husband to relocate again. He found a job there as a "repo-man"—retrieving cars from customers unable to make their promised monthly payments. To supplement his income, Paul bought, restored, and sold old cars. The Jobs' garage was always packed with tools and full of potential.

The call from the San Francisco doctor nearly sent the couple into orbit. Due to the circumstances of the initial failed placement, Paul and Clara had no warning and little time to react. They were ecstatic, though, and gleefully accepted. However, when Joanne found out neither Paul nor Clara had a college education, she was furious and refused to sign the relinquishment papers. Days turned to weeks. Finally, after receiving assurance through the doctor the Jobs would send Steve to college, Joanne agreed to finalize the placement.

LIKE FATHER, LIKE SON

The Jobs settled into a rhythm as a family of three. When Steve turned two, they adopted again, this time a newborn girl named Patty. Paul continued his work repossessing cars. When Steve turned five, the Jobs purchased a single-story ranch house at 2066 Crist Drive in Los Altos. It was inside the garage of that simple suburban home where Steve Jobs began to sow the seeds of his future destiny. Steve's father marked off a portion of his workbench for his young son. He shared his love of cars with him and encouraged him to tinker and explore.

"I wasn't that into fixing cars," Steve would later say, "But I was eager to hang out with my dad."[2]

It was an impressionable time. "I thought my dad's sense of design was pretty good," Jobs said. "He knew how to build anything. If we needed a cabinet, he would build it. When we built our fence, he gave me a hammer so I could work with him. He loved doing things right. He even cared about the look of the parts you couldn't see."[3] Although Steve didn't embrace his father's love of automobile mechanics, his father first introduced him to electronics, given the critical role they played in the car. "He showed me the rudiments of electronics and I got very interested in that. Every weekend, there'd be a junkyard trip. We'd be looking for a generator, a carburetor, all sorts of components."[4]

NEIGHBORHOOD INFLUENCE

Paul and Clara Jobs worked tirelessly to feed the interests of their children, especially Steve's. Clara taught him how to read before he even started kindergarten. The location of the Jobs' home placed the youngster squarely in the middle of the exploding tech boom. "Most of the dads in the neighborhood did really neat stuff, like photovoltaics and batteries and radar," Jobs remembered. One of those fathers, Larry Lang, who lived just seven houses down, was an engineer for Hewlett Packard (HP). "He would bring me stuff to play with," said Jobs.[5] A fourth grade teacher, Imogene Hill, gave Steve a Heathkit, a tool that fed his love of electronics. He would later call her "one of the saints in my life."[6]

Conversations around the table inevitably turned technical, especially when Steve's father took a new job with Spectra-Physics, a company that engineered lasers. A young Steve was impressed with his father's new profession. "Lasers require precision alignment," he said. "The really sophisticated ones, for airborne applications or medical, had very precise features. It made you realize you could build and understand anything. Once you built a couple of radios, you'd see a TV in the catalogue and say, 'I can build that as well,' even if you didn't. I was very lucky, because when I was a kid both my dad and the Heathkits[7] made me believe I could build anything."[8]

The Jobs' decision to buy in the Mountain View section of Los Altos also wound up exposing Steve to the architecture of Joseph Eichler, a real estate developer whose company built more than eleven thousand homes in California. Eichler's homes were designed for the average American. "Eichler did a great thing," Jobs told his biographer. "His houses were smart and cheap and good. They brought clean design and simple taste to lower income people. They had awesome little features like radiant heating in the floors. You put carpet on them and we had nice toasty floors. I love it when you can bring really great design and simple capability to something that doesn't cost much. It was the original vision of Apple. That's what we tried to do with the first Mac. That's what we did with the iPod."[9]

Paul Jobs also encouraged his son to accept Larry Lang's invitation to join the Hewlett-Packard Explorers Club, a group of students who met weekly in the company cafeteria. Steve recalled the experience:

> They would get an engineer from one of the labs to come talk about what he was working on. My dad would drive me there. I was in heaven. I saw my first desktop computer there.... It was huge, maybe forty pounds, but it was a beauty of a thing. I fell in love with it.[10]

When a group project required parts Steve didn't have, he decided, on his own, to call Bill Hewlett, the CEO of HP. He simply looked up his number in the phone book. They had a twenty-minute conversation. Steve not only received the parts he was looking for but Bill wound up offering him a summer internship. He eagerly accepted.

"MY PARENTS MADE ME FEEL SPECIAL"

In the opening pages of his biography, Steve Jobs reflected candidly on his adoption. He always knew he was adopted. "My parents were very open with me about that," he told Walter Isaacson.[11] But he recalls a chilling moment when he was maybe six or seven years of age. He told the girl across the street that he was adopted, to which she replied, "So does that mean your real parents didn't want you?"

"Lightning bolts went off in my head," he said. "I remember running into the house, crying. And my parents said, 'No, you have to understand.' They were very serious and looked me straight in the eye. They said, 'We specifically picked you out.' Both of my parents said that and repeated it slowly for me. And they put an emphasis on every word in that sentence."[12]

Responding to critics who suggest Jobs' career and personal behavior bore the mark of a man still struggling with abandonment, Steve adamantly disagreed. "Knowing I was adopted may have made me feel more independent, but I have never felt abandoned. I've always felt special. My parents made me feel special."[13] And to those who inadvertently or ignorantly suggested his adoptive mom and dad weren't his "real" parents, Steve was quick to clarify: "They were my parents. 1000%."[14]

THE REST OF THE STORY

Steve Jobs' biological parents, Joanne Schieble and Abdulfattah Jandali, married shortly after Steve's adoption. They divorced in 1962. The marriage resulted in the birth of another child, a daughter, the bestselling novelist Mona Simpson. It would take twenty years before Steve and Mona eventually met, but they quickly forged a powerful bond. Jobs declined an invitation to meet his biological father, but warmly embraced the opportunity to meet his biological mother.

"I wanted to meet [her] mostly to see if she was okay and to thank her, because I'm glad I didn't end up as an abortion," he said. "She was twenty-three and she went through a lot to have me."[15]

Steve's reluctance to meet Mr. Jandali was born out of concern the restaurateur would blackmail him or make an appeal for money. Ironically, the restaurant Jandali operated was often frequented by Silicon Valley executives, including Steve Jobs. At the time, though, Jandali was not aware who his first born son was or what had become of him.

Paul and Clara Jobs were married for just over forty years. Clara passed away in 1986. Paul died in 1993.

Every adoption is the culmination of countless independent decisions the Lord seamlessly works together. Some might scoff at the suggestion Steve Jobs accomplished what he did in large part because he was adopted by Paul and Clara Jobs, but the evidence suggests otherwise: that Joanne Schieble chose not to have an abortion—that the young Wisconsin woman was referred to a California doctor who just happened to be the same doctor the Jobs petitioned—that the first couple matched declined because they wanted a girl not a boy—that Joanne agreed to place with the Jobs despite their lack of college education—that Paul and Clara both lived and worked where they did, surrounded by the sultans of science and engineering—and that they nurtured, navigated, and loved an exceptionally gifted but challenging boy from childhood to the heights of professional success.

Adoption didn't necessarily make Steve Jobs successful, but it undoubtedly shaped the man who co-founded the company that has changed the way we compute and communicate.

"Once, he told me," said his sister Mona Simpson, "if he'd grown up differently, he might have become a mathematician."[16]

IN SEARCH OF WONDER

Spiritually speaking, it's impossible to know what goes on inside a man's heart. History is replete with dramatic deathbed conversions. According to those present in Palo Alto, there was no such moment or declaration in Steve Jobs' final days. However, his final words, spoken haltingly but clearly, are provocative.

Mona Simpson revealed at his funeral that after making eye contact with everyone in the room, Jobs turned and gazed beyond them, as if looking at a scene unfolding over their shoulders. "Oh wow!" he said. "Oh, wow! Oh, wow!"[17]

What did he see? It's impossible to know. But it's fitting that the man whose life's work revolved around the pursuit of rethinking man's approach to the wonder of technology is the same man whose last words were wrapped in the spirit of wonder itself.

CHAPTER TWO

NANCY REAGAN

A nne Francis Robbins was a young woman on a mission.

In the summer of 1935, at just past 9:30 in the morning and after a sixteen-hour trip from Chicago, the weary and anxious fourteen-year-old stepped slowly off the New York Central Railroad's famed 20th Century Limited train. She made her way up the long stone staircase beneath East 42nd Street and into the cavernous main concourse of Grand Central Station. Long, brilliant rays of sunshine streamed through the upper windows of the building. The auburn-haired teenager weaved her way through the shafts of light as her fellow travelers hurriedly crisscrossed four different ways across the sparkling marbled pavilion.

Anne, known affectionately by her family and friends as "Nancy," traveled from her home on Lake Shore Drive in Chicago to visit with her biological father, Kenneth Robbins, and her grandmother, Anna. They agreed to meet under the large golden clock inside the Palm Court of the Biltmore Hotel, a neo-classical structure directly across the street from the train station. Ever since Nancy's parents separated just prior to her birth, ultimately divorcing six years later, she and Kenneth met each summer, though as she aged, the visits grew less frequent.

But this occasion was neither social nor ordinary.

Nancy requested to see her birth father in the hope he would be willing to sign papers relinquishing his paternal rights, thereby allowing his only daughter to be adopted by her stepfather, Dr. Loyal Davis, a prominent Chicago neurosurgeon.

How she arrived at this moment of decision is a story of many twists and turns.

THE EARLY DAYS

Nancy's mother, Edith Luckett, was the youngest of nine children. The Washington, D.C., family struggled to make ends meet and many of Edith's siblings quit school early in order to help pay the bills. Providentially, Joseph, her oldest brother, took a job managing a local theater. When Edith turned sixteen, Joseph gave his youngest sister her first opportunity to perform on stage. She loved it. In an instant, Edith found her life's ambition.

Nancy's birth father, Kenneth Robbins, was born in Pittsfield, Massachusetts. Although he claimed to have graduated from Princeton University, official records suggest otherwise. The son of a manufacturing executive, Kenneth was working as a shoe salesman when he and Edith met in 1914. They married two years later. Admittedly less ambitious than his new wife, Robbins agreed to relocate to New York so Edith could find acting work. However, he despised the hustle and bustle of the city, and their marriage floundered from its earliest days. He struggled to find a good fit for work. Kenneth took a position as a talent booking agent, but failed to gain any momentum, once joking his only two clients were "a one-legged tap dancer and a cross-eyed knife thrower."[1] It would be the first of his many unsuccessful attempts at a career.

When the United States entered World War I in 1917, Kenneth eagerly enlisted in the Army. When he returned after the war in 1919, his and Edith's struggles began anew. He tried his hand in real estate sales and even auto mechanics. Both were miserable failures. He finally found some measure of success selling automobiles.

So, when Nancy was born on July 6, 1921, in Queens, a borough of New York City, the Robbins' marriage was already on the rocks. Out of desperation, Kenneth had left Edith to go back up to Pittsfield. At the time, his wife was just three months pregnant. He bounced back and forth between Massachusetts and New York for the first year of Nancy's life, but the separation soon became permanent. "I was told later that my father wasn't at the hospital when I was born," Nancy recalled. "[That] must have hurt Mother as much as it did me when I heard about it.... He was my father, but I somehow never could think of him that way because there had never been any relationship of any kind."[2]

MOVING SOUTH

With Kenneth now living with his mother in Massachusetts, Edith found life as a single mother difficult, if not impossible. Shortly before Nancy turned two, she made the decision to ask her sister Virginia and brother-in-law Audley Galbraith if her daughter might live with them in their Bethesda, Maryland, home. The couple, who had one daughter, agreed. What was originally thought to be just a short stay eventually become a nearly six-year season of discontent for the future first lady of the United States.

After dropping off Nancy, Edith returned to New York City, rented a room on West 49th Street and resumed her acting career, landing back with the same traveling stock company with whom she worked prior to Nancy's arrival. Edith took every opportunity possible to see her daughter, but the nature of her work often resulted in long gaps between visits. Responding to critics who speculated how Edith could have decided upon such an arrangement, Kitty Kelly, the gossip columnist and author of an unauthorized biography on Nancy Reagan, said her mother "could never quite shake the stardust of the stage."[3]

The separation was painful for both mother and daughter. Speaking to Susan Crosland of the *Sunday Times* of London, Nancy reflected on the trauma of those years. "The early childhood certainly left its mark," she said. "But everything leaves its mark on you. Doesn't it? I'm not terribly good at psychoanalyzing myself."[4] Still, those closest to Nancy report she felt abandoned twice over, first by the father she really never knew and then by the mother she only saw on rare, special occasions.

Nancy's birth father Kenneth soon relocated with his mother to Verona, New Jersey. The proximity to Maryland made it possible for him to see his daughter for a short visit each summer. But the damage from that early separation made it difficult for the two of them to connect on a deep level. "He (my birthfather) couldn't relate to me as a very young child," Nancy remembered. "But as I grew older and became more of a person, he'd want to see me more."[5] However, Nancy wasn't too keen on seeing him. Their visits became more irregular after a particularly difficult incident. "He once made a disparaging remark about Mother," Nancy remembered. "I no longer recall what it was—which enraged me to the point where I screamed at him that I wanted to leave. He got upset and locked me in the bathroom. I was terrified, and I suddenly felt as if I were with strangers."[6]

THE TIDE TURNS

Though terribly missing her mother, Nancy embraced the relative stability of life with her aunt and uncle in the small but tidy house on Glenbrook Road in Bethesda, Maryland. Beginning in kindergarten, she attended the Sidwell Friends School, a private Quaker institution. She made friends easily. The school's motto, "Eluceat omnibus lux" or "Let the light shine out from all," foreshadowed the life young Nancy would soon enjoy.

Meanwhile, up in Chicago, Nancy's mother was performing alongside a young Spencer Tracy in George M. Cohan's play, *The Baby Cyclone*. It was to be just another stop in just another city, but when Edith met a young neurosurgeon in the audience named Loyal Davis, her world was turned upside down.

At the time of their meeting, Dr. Davis was associate professor of experimental surgery at Northwestern University in Chicago. At just thirty-three years of age, Davis was a rising star. A previous marriage, which resulted in the birth of a son, had recently ended in divorce. Nevertheless, Edith and Loyal, both eager for love and companionship, immediately began dating. The romance took off like a rocket. Edith, though, wary of how Nancy would react to them getting married, found her way to Maryland to talk with her about their relationship. "I won't marry Dr. Davis unless you think I should," she told her young daughter.[7] Nancy gave her consent. Loyal and Edith were married on May 21, 1929, in a small chapel of the Fourth Presbyterian Church in Chicago.

Following the wedding, however, Nancy wrestled with mixed emotions. On the one hand, what she had been dreaming about and praying for—reunification with her mother and a traditional home life—had finally come true. On the other hand, she was nervous about abandoning the familiar rhythms and routines of life on the East Coast.

Her natural instincts proved prescient.

Looking back on the transition from her aunt and uncle's house in Bethesda to Chicago, Nancy said her new stepfather seemed to be "formal and distant, and at first I resented having to share my mother with him. I was jealous of their close relationship."[8] Fortunately, Dr. Davis sensed the discomfort. "He allowed me to come to know him at my own pace," Nancy later said.[9] In time the relationship improved.

After the wedding, Edith landed a role on *The Betty and Bob Show*, a national radio soap opera on NBC. The substantial income from the position (between $500 and $1,000 a month) helped supplement the rather modest earnings of her new husband. Although a well-respected doctor, his income paled in comparison to that of an entertainer. Shortly thereafter, however, she quit the theater and instead turned her full attention to creating a home for her husband and resuming her duties as a full-time mother to Nancy. For an outlet and showing something of an entrepreneurial spirit, Edith started the gift shop at Passavant Hospital (now Northwestern Memorial Hospital) where her new husband was working. Friends of the newlyweds recall the dedication and devotion Edith demonstrated. "When Edie married Loyal," said the late Lester Weinrott, "she was like Michelangelo looking at the Sistine Chapel for the first time. She was going to create herself a masterpiece."[10]

Mr. Weinrott goes on to describe the practical benefits of Loyal and Edith's union. "Loyal had the credentials and she had the moxie," he said. "They both got a good deal when they married each other. He got himself a dynamo who would pay the bills and introduce him to the right people, and she got a security blanket for herself and her daughter. Without Edie, Loyal would never have made it in Chicago. Without him, she wouldn't have been accepted. She was determined to make him the most prestigious physician in the city and get them into the Social Register, which she felt would pave the way for Nancy to be a lady of social graces."[11]

FATHER KNOWS BEST

After the initial challenges surrounding the transition from Maryland to Chicago, eight-year-old Nancy began to settle into life in the Windy City. Her parents enrolled her in the Girls' Latin School of Chicago, a private and prestigious institution. She also began making lifetime friendships. Her best friend, Jean Wescott Marshall, once told the biographer Bob Colacello that she and Nancy especially enjoyed going to the movies together in high school. "We were all wrapped up in movie stars," she said. "I liked Ronald Reagan, and she liked Bing Crosby. She used to say, 'I don't see what you see in Ronald Reagan.'"[12]

Nancy quickly bonded with her new stepfather. "Loyal Davis," she would later say, "was a man of integrity who exemplified old-fashioned values: That girls and boys should grow up to be ladies and gentlemen. That children should respect and obey their parents. That no matter what you did, you should never cheapen yourself. And that whatever you worked at—whether it was a complicated medical procedure, or a relatively simple act like sweeping the floor—you should do it as well as you could."[13]

Within medical circles, Loyal Davis was considered both a maverick and a world renowned brain surgeon. He was an honorary fellow of the

Royal College in Edinburgh, Scotland, and the Royal College of Surgeons in London. For more than twenty-five years he both wrote and served as editor of the journal *Surgery, Gynecology and Obstetrics*. A stickler for protocols and procedures, he once caused a national stir by asserting that half of the surgeries in the United States were being performed by doctors unqualified for operating rooms. During World War II, he served in the Army as a doctor in Europe, devising a helmet to protect pilots from shrapnel and also improved the treatment for high-altitude frostbite.

POLITICAL INFLUENCE

But in addition to his medical prowess, when it came to politics, Loyal Davis had a reputation for having strong conservative opinions. He was an active member in the John Birch Society. Conversations at the Davis dinner table regularly dealt with issues and candidates. He believed and preached personal responsibility and the freedom of every person to pursue their own dreams without the interference of government. Nancy credited Loyal with helping her cultivate, clarify, and solidify her own political convictions.

Some have even credited Dr. Davis with helping to convert Nancy's future husband and the fortieth president of the United States, Ronald Reagan, from liberal Democrat to conservative Republican.

Is it true?

Such a claim would appear to be somewhat exaggerated though at the very least, there's little doubt Dr. Davis's influence would have helped to shore up the president's evolving commitment to conservative ideals at an especially critical time in his life. When the fledgling actor and Nancy met in 1951, Reagan was still a registered Democrat and had, just a year earlier, campaigned for Helen Gahagan Douglas in her bid for the U.S. Senate against Richard Nixon. Although his role with General Electric in the 1950s caused him to begin questioning the government's increasingly burdensome role in American lives, Reagan wouldn't officially change his party registration from Democrat to Republican until 1962. It was during that same decade, however, when Mr. Reagan would sit and chat with Dr.

Davis for hours about politics and life in general. The surgeon despised socialized medicine and was suspicious of any government involvement in medicine. Ronald Reagan was listening and absorbing.

THE DECISION TO ADOPT

Since Nancy's biological father was still living at the time Dr. Davis and Edith married in 1929, Loyal felt uncomfortable with the idea of officially adopting his new stepdaughter. That's because to do so would require Nancy's biological father, Kenneth, to forever relinquish his parental rights. But as time went on and Nancy grew closer and closer to her stepfather, she felt herself growing further and further apart from her biological dad. "He tried to please me," she acknowledged, "but too many years had gone by, and we were really strangers."[14] Both the physical and emotional distance left her with an intense longing to officially belong and share her new family's name. She felt a certain stigma with the blended family. "I have always hated being referred to as the 'step-daughter' of Loyal Davis," she once said. "To this day, I can't stand that word 'step.'"[15]

So when Nancy became friendly with a retired judge who lived in the apartment adjacent to the Davis family in Chicago, she asked the neighbor what it would take for her stepfather to adopt her. The judge explained the process. Nancy became excited at the prospect and expressed her wishes to both Edith and Loyal. They agreed contingent upon Kenneth Robbins's willingness to agree to Nancy's request. The papers were drawn up and a trip to New York was planned.

By the summer of 1935, Kenneth Davis, who remarried in 1928, was selling cars in New Jersey and managing a fledging dealership. They lived a simple life inside a country home in the rural town of Sparta. When Kenneth received Nancy's request to meet, he decided to bring Nancy's grandmother along with him to the Biltmore Hotel. The reunion was cordial. "I explained what I wanted to do," remembered Nancy. "And they agreed, reluctantly."[16]

With the relinquishment papers in hand, a relieved and exuberant Nancy made a beeline for a telegraph office. "I sent a wire to Chicago to tell my family that the adoption had gone through," she said. "I didn't have much experience with telegrams, but I knew they had to be brief. This one read: HI DAD."

LEADING LADY

For a teenage Nancy, her adoption into the Davis family lifted an enormous psychological weight from her shoulders. No longer did she feel like an outcast or fifth wheel. At long last she had a father both in name and in reality, a dad in whom she could confide, receive counsel, and most importantly, develop the confidence that would propel her toward a public life on the world's largest stage. When she returned to school following the finalization of her adoption in 1935, her friends remembered how excited she was to announce her new name.

Nancy Davis would go on to attend and study drama at Smith College. Following in her mother's footsteps, she joined a touring company and eventually landed a minor role in the Broadway musical *Lute Song*. In 1949, she was given a seven-year contract with MGM studios and began appearing in motion pictures. When another actress named Nancy Davis was suspected of being a communist sympathizer, a friend recommended that she meet with Ronald Reagan, then the president of the Screen Actors Guild. In his role, Reagan would be in a position to help her clear up the confusion. He did. That fateful meeting would, of course, lead to a storied fifty-two-year marriage taking the Reagans to the heights of worldly power and influence.

Ronald Reagan's two terms as governor of California (1968–1976) and two terms as president of the United States (1981–1989) provided Nancy with two roles the first lady relished, but none more so than that of being Reagan's wife. "My life didn't begin until I met Ronnie," she once said.[17] In return, the fortieth president replied, "I can't imagine life without her."[18]

ADOPTION AS THE TURNING POINT

Almost every account of Nancy Reagan's life makes a brief mention of her adoption, but very little about the impact it had on the next eighty years of her life. Yet, in reviewing the records and circumstances surrounding the pivotal decision of her stepfather to adopt her, it would be impossible to overstate its significance. Her adoption in 1935 provided her with a mother and father and the stability and security Nancy craved since her birth in 1921. The resources of the Davis family made it possible for Nancy to receive an excellent education and pursue the dreams and aspirations God placed on her heart.

When Nancy Reagan passed away on March 6, 2016, at the age of ninety-four, she was lauded for her tenacity and devotion to her husband. She was also remembered for her courage and the confidence with which she so publicly served. Years earlier, the late Michael Deaver, a longtime aide to the Reagans, suggested, "Without Nancy, there would have been no Governor Reagan, no President Reagan."[19]

But have you ever thought of this?

Without a Loyal Davis, the adoptive father of Nancy, a man who arrived in Edith Robbins's life at just the right moment, there also would never have been an innocent actress named Nancy Davis needing to speak with a fledgling actor named Ronald Reagan.

CHAPTER THREE

NELSON MANDELA

When Nelson Mandela died on December 5, 2013, at the age of ninety-five, a leading newspaper in Great Britain suggested one would have to go back to the assassination of President Kennedy in 1963 in order "to find a comparable occasion of collective [worldwide] bereavement."[1]

Similar tributes rolled in from all corners of the globe.

Bill Keller of the *New York Times* eulogized the anti-apartheid activist who became the first president of a democratic South Africa as a "rarity among revolutionaries and moral dissidents: a capable statesman, comfortable with compromise and impatient with the doctrinaire."[2] Former President George H. W. Bush hailed the 1993 Nobel Prize winner as a leader who set "a powerful example of redemption and grace...a man of tremendous moral courage, who changed the course of history in his country."[3]

In a tear-filled address to the same people Mr. Mandela once led, current South African President Jacob Zuma made the emotional declaration that "Our nation has lost its greatest son."[4] And in a joint statement from the president of the European Commission, Jose Manuel Barroso and the president of the European Council, Herman Van Rompuy, Mr. Mandela was described as a leader who "represented the fight against racism, political violence and intolerance."[5]

Indeed, the life and legacy of Nelson Mandela are a remarkable tale of a magnanimous yet imperfect man on an unconventional and nearly impossible journey. How does a young boy from a polygamous family in a tiny village emerge from twenty-seven years of wrongful imprisonment to finally emancipate his nation?

As is the case so often, Mr. Mandela's triumphant story began amidst tragedy and heartbreak.

THE BOY FROM MVEZO

He was born Rolihlahla Dalibunga Mphakanyiswa on July 18, 1918, in the rolling hills of the district of Mtata, the capital of the Transkei in South Africa and home of the Xhosa Nation. His biological father was Gadla Hendry Mphakanyiswa, a chief of the Thembu/Mvezo people. To celebrate his son's birth, Gadla slaughtered a goat and mounted the animal's horns on the hut.

When he was seven years old, Rolihlahla received the name of "Nelson" (likely after Lord Nelson, the famous British admiral) from a teacher in the missionary school he began attending. In the white-dominated world of South Africa, it was common for black youngsters to be given easier-to-pronounce English names by their teachers. By all accounts he readily embraced it, though his parents did not. His father chose the name Rolihlahla, which meant "pulling the branch of a tree"—or "troublemaker"—and refused to call him by his new name.

Nelson's biological mother was Nosekeni Fanny, the third (concurrent) wife of Mphakanyiswa, who would eventually have four children by Nelson's father. In addition to caring for the children (Nelson had nine sisters and three brothers), Nosekeni farmed and raised livestock. Poverty was a way of life. For the first seven years of his life, Nelson wore only a blanket pinned at his waist. When he began attending school, though, his father insisted he dress more professionally. Gadla took a pair of his own trousers, cut them at the knee and showed Nelson how he could use a rope to cinch them at his waist. "I must have been a comical sight," he would later say. "But I have never owned a suit I was prouder to wear than my father's cut off trousers."[6]

The family's routine and its future began to change in 1926 when Nelson's father ran into trouble with the local white colonial magistrate. According to Nelson's telling, the dispute stemmed from a simple misunderstanding concerning a stray ox. When Gadla refused to accept the ruling, he was charged with insubordination and relieved of his duties as chief. "My father possessed a proud rebelliousness," recalled Mandela, "a stubborn sense of fairness that I recognize in myself."[7] Researchers would later uncover documentation that Gadla had actually been charged with corruption and abuse of power.

Regardless of the actual reason for the dismissal, the now discredited Gadla moved his family to the small village of Qunu for a fresh start. The change of location suited the eight-year-old Nelson very well. Reflecting on the area's influence he would later write: "It was in the fields that I learned how to knock birds out of the sky with a slingshot, to gather wild honey and fruit and edible roots, to drink warm, sweet milk from the udder of a cow, to swim in the clear, cold streams, and to catch fish with twine and sharpened bits of wire."[8]

THE RISE TO ROYALTY

Nelson's seemingly idyllic life was shattered a year later when his father died of what was likely tuberculosis, though it was never officially diagnosed. Ill for an extended period of time and burdened for the future of his son, Gadla Mphakanyiswa approached his friend, Jongintaba Dalindyebo. Dalindyebo was the high-ranking regent and supreme chief of the Thembu people. Would he be willing to adopt Nelson and raise him as one of his own? Nelson's father had a strong sense that his son was destined to do something significant. "I can see from the way he speaks to his sisters and friends," he assuring Dalindyebo, "that his inclination is to help the nation."[9] The chief readily and enthusiastically agreed. He would consider it an honor to welcome the nine-year-old Nelson into their home.

What about his biological mother, Nosekeni Fanny? Why wouldn't he just live with her? Here we see evidence of the drastic divide of cultures, the contradiction of personal values, and yet the innate and instinctual desires of every boy to bond with a father figure. Partly because of the polygamous society in which he lived and partly because of the patriarchal nature of the times, Nelson never felt especially close to his biological father. In fact, although he strongly desired his companionship, he saw very little of him. At the same time, he spent nearly all his time with one of the four mothers in his family. He would later acknowledge that while such a clan of women caring for him was comforting, he considered polygamy to be an abuse of women.

But now, his father was dead, and while conflicted with competing emotions, the idea of joining the Dalindyebos appealed to him. Though grieving his loss, he saw his adoption as an opportunity for his wildest dreams to come true—to grow up with a strong and involved father as well as receive the education his small village could not offer. "Although my mother was the centre of my existence," he confessed, "I defined myself through my father."[10] He came to consider the move as a turning point. "My father's passing changed my whole life in a way that I did not suspect at the time. Suddenly, a new world opened before me. In that instant, I saw that life might hold more for me than being a champion stick fighter."[11]

But at the time of his father's death, Nelson knew none of this. All he knew was he was leaving the village and saying good-bye to everything familiar. His mother filled a small tin trunk with a few of his possessions and together they started off. She didn't tell him where he was going. He didn't ask.

"Before we disappeared behind the hills," he wrote, "I turned and looked for what I imagined was the last time at my village. Above all else, my eyes rested on the three simple huts where I had enjoyed my mother's love and protection. It was these three huts that I associated with all my happiness, with life itself, and I rued the fact that I had not kissed each of them before I left. I could not imagine that the future I was walking toward could compare in any way to the past that I was leaving behind."[12] Mother and son walked all day, rarely saying a word. By sunset they arrived.

His life would never again be the same.

FORWARD INTO THE FUTURE

Arriving in Mqhekezweni, otherwise known as the "Great Place," Nelson found himself in a drastically different environment than the modest mud huts of his previous home. At the center of the village stood a grand, stately house, a structure unlike anything Nelson had ever seen. "All I could do was marvel at it," he remembered. In addition to the mansion, he saw two rectangular buildings and seven rondavels (huts) washed in white limestone, that, according to his memory, were "dazzling in the light of the setting sun."[13]

Nelson's mother stayed for a few days, just long enough for him to get settled. She worked hard to avoid showing any emotion. "She offered no sermons, no words of wisdom, no kisses. . . . As she departed she turned to me and said, 'Uqinisufokotho, kwedini!'—'Brace yourself, my boy!'"[14]

In addition to serving as Chief Jongintaba Dalindyebo's base of operations, Mqhekezweni was also a Methodist mission station. Unlike his biological father, Dalindyebo was a devout Christian, and Nelson began attending weekly church services. In his previous village, any reference to faith was purely ritualistic. His biological father didn't practice anything and his mother, while a professing Christian, didn't incorporate it into the daily lives of the family. The only time Nelson ever attended church in Qunu was the day he was baptized in a Wesleyan chapel. At Mqhekezweni, however, Christianity defined and shaped not only his daily life, but also the entire community that surrounded and supported him.

"The two principles that governed my life at Mqhekezweni," Mandela wrote, "were chieftancy and the Church. These two doctrines existed in uneasy harmony, although I did not then see them as antagonistic. For me, Christianity was not so much a system of beliefs as it was the powerful creed of a single man, Reverend Matyolo. For me, his powerful presence embodied all that was alluring in Christianity."[15] As a young Christian, Nelson appreciated the practical nature of the Christian faith. "The Church was as concerned with this world as the next. I saw that virtually all of the achievements of Africans seemed to have come through the missionary work of the Church."[16]

At the time of Nelson's arrival, the Reverend Matyolo was in his mid fifties and had a reputation for delivering fire and brimstone sermons. People came in droves to hear his deep, sonorous voice. "The hall rang with the hosannas of the faithful," Mandela remembered.[17] Impressed with Matyolo's ability to both sing and preach with equal fervor, Nelson's faith grew by leaps and bounds during his ten years there.

As a disciplinarian, the pastor was tough but fair and got along well with everyone. The curriculum of the adjacent church-run school provided an additional dose of a Christian worldview. Classes in English, history, Xhosa (one of the official languages of South Africa) and geography were taught. By all accounts, Nelson was a diligent and serious student. In fact, due to the soberness of his temperament, many of his friends called him "Tatomkhulu"—grandpa.

LIKE ONE OF THEIR OWN

Nelson Mandela's adopted father, Chief Jongintaba, was married to No-England, a kind and gracious woman with whom Mandela would bond. His arrival added to their family by a third. Justice was the oldest brother, followed by a daughter named Nomafu. If Nelson was serious, Justice was the polar opposite. Those who knew him well qualified Nelson's older new brother as being cheerful and outgoing—even "something of a playboy." Yet the differences didn't negatively impact his ability to grow accustomed to family life. Mandela later said his new parents made him feel immediately welcome. "They brought me up as if I were their own child. They worried about me, guided me, and punished me, all in a spirit of fairness."[18] According to Nelson, his new father was "stern" but stressed, "I never doubted his love."[19]

The years at Mqhekezweni were also formative in ways beyond faith and family. Nelson became a student of his new father's managerial style. He was impressed with his collaborative and humble approach, acknowledging, "My later notions of leadership were profoundly influenced by observing [my father] and his court. I watched and learned from the tribal meetings that were regularly held at the Great Place."[20]

Among the more profound takeaways would be his first exposure to true democracy and a commitment, whenever possible, to finding consensus. "A minority was not to be crushed by a majority," he would say.[21] Nelson also came to appreciate the importance of listening before speaking and as a leader guiding a discussion, waiting to offer an opinion before inviting everyone to first offer their own perspective.

At Mqhekezweni, his father's Christian faith was clearly manifest, believing a leader is to be like a shepherd guiding his sheep. "He stays behind his flock," stressed Mandela, "letting the most nimble go out ahead, whereupon the others follow, not realizing all along they are being directed from behind."[22] He also learned the importance of developing thick skin and not taking everything personally. "At first," he said, "I was astonished by the vehemence—and candor—with which people criticized my father. He was not above criticism—in fact, he was often the principal target of it. But no matter how flagrant the charge, my father simply listened, not defending himself, showing no emotion at all."[23]

TURNING FROM TRIBAL TRADITIONS

When Nelson Mandela turned sixteen, his father enrolled him in Clarebury Institute in Engcobo. There the headmaster was another strong Christian, the Reverend Harris. Mandela was told he had a love for the Tembu people. The transition was a point of celebration for the family, and a sheep was slaughtered to mark the occasion. Nelson also received his first pair of formal shoes, which he found a bit challenging to wear. "I walked like a horse in spurs," he would recall with laughter.[24]

Outside his village for the first time in ten years, Mandela had his first real exposure to the ongoing racial tensions between his fellow blacks and the white ruling class. Because of his inexperience, though, he found it difficult to fully appreciate the emotions attached to racial conflict. In fact, some have suggested this naiveté helped him cultivate the cool temperament that helped sustain him during his years of imprisonment.

While Clarebury was often the final stop for many students, Nelson's father, eager to maximize his son's opportunities, enrolled him in Healdtown—a prime black school in South Africa. Drawn to the solitude of the sport, Mandela became a competitive long-distance runner. He also began boxing. Nelson excelled academically, but credits the visit of the Xhosa writer, poet, and singer Krune Mqhayi with opening his mind to what later came to be the mission and magnificent obsession of his life.

Standing before the students in the assembly hall in full Xhosa dress, Mqhayi read some of his politically provocative poetry, and with a dramatic flair, prophesied the day was coming when oppressed black Africans would once again regain their freedom and dignity. "I could hardly believe my ears," Mandela wrote in his autobiography, "His boldness in speaking of such delicate matters in the presence of Dr. Wellington (the headmaster) and other whites seemed utterly astonishing to us. Yet, at the same time, it aroused and motivated us."[25] According to Mandela, that one visit in 1938 "seemed to turn the universe upside down."[26] Indeed, it had planted a seed. For the first time in his life, he no longer saw all of the white authorities as his benefactors, but realized many of them were holding him back.

From Healdtown, Mandela enrolled in the University of Fort Hale—the equivalent of an American Ivy League school for black South Africans. His intellect and world were expanding exponentially, but his time at the school was short-lived.

At the end of his first year, Mandela was nominated to run for one of the six seats on the Student Representative Council. He was well liked and thriving. At the time, the student body was upset with the poor food the school was serving and wanted the administration to expand the powers of the Council so they could help fix the problem. School officials disagreed. In protest, many of the students, Mandela included, boycotted the election, thinking they outsmarted the administration.

Since the school's constitution required the whole student body to vote, Mandela and his peers contended the election was therefore illegitimate. And although Mandela was elected, he and the other five students immediately resigned their posts. In response, the school's principal decided to hold another election the next day during dinner—contending the whole student body was thus present to vote. With the same outcome, Mandela's five classmates accepted the results—but Nelson could not. "I had taken a stand," he said, "and I did not want to appear to be a fraud in the eyes of my fellow students."[27]

The principal asked him to reconsider and gave him until the next day, threatening expulsion if he didn't accept the results of the election. A conflicted Mandela held his ground. Looking to avoid a showdown and since it was the end of the semester, the principal offered him the summer to change his mind. But the break only strengthened his convictions.

In September, Nelson Mandela was officially expelled from the University of Fort Hale. Years later he called his actions "foolhardy."

RESOLVED AND READY FOR TOMORROW

Back home at the Great Place in Mqhekezweni, Mandela's father announced to him that in keeping with tribal tradition he arranged for his son to marry the daughter of a local priest. His brother Justice, who was now living in Capetown, was to marry the daughter of a Thembu aristocrat. All the arrangements were made, including the price for the two brides. The wedding was to take place immediately.

But neither Nelson nor Justice wanted to marry at that point, let alone to women their father chose. They knew full well the customs of the tribe, but pleaded with their father to reconsider. Nelson even went so far as to blame his father for his "progressive" beliefs, citing the influence of all the schooling he and Justice had received since leaving home.

The chief wouldn't budge, so Nelson and his brother did the only thing they felt they could do: they ran away from home and resettled in Johannesburg. To pay for their journey, they stole two oxen from their father, and managed to use some connections and persuasion to avoid apprehension. Along with a partner there, Nelson would eventually open the first black law office in the country.

For Mandela, the arrival in South Africa's largest city would become a turning point in a life only getting started, though he didn't fully appreciate the significance of his decision at the time. "I had reached the end of what seemed like a long journey," he would later write, "but it was actually the very beginning of a much longer and more trying journey that would test me in ways that I could not then have imagined."[28]

THE REST OF THE STORY

From his auspicious arrival in Johannesburg in 1941, Nelson Mandela's involvement in liberation politics quickly grew, especially after the end of World War II in 1945. He married Evelyn Ntoke Mase and together they had four children. They struggled with their marriage, exacerbated when Evelyn became a Jehovah's Witness. They eventually divorced.

Nelson continued to pursue his work in his law practice, but when the National Party officially legislated Apartheid in 1948—separating whites from blacks in all areas of life—he became active in the African National Congress, even heading up its youth movement.

From the beginning, in pursuing equality, Mandela always preached peace, but after sixty-nine black demonstrators were killed in 1961, he decided it was necessary to switch to more militant tactics. "There is no moral goodness," he said, "in using an ineffective weapon."[29] Historians suggest that much of his activity has been mythologized. But there's little doubt he was caught up in the movement. For his activities and conspiracy, he was arrested and convicted twice, the second time for attempting to commit sabotage against the South African government.

"During my lifetime I have dedicated myself to this struggle of the African people," he said on the eve of his imprisonment. "I have fought against white domination, and I have fought against black domination. I have cherished the ideal of a democratic and free society in which all persons live together in harmony and with equal opportunities. It is an ideal which I hope to live for and to achieve. But if need be, it is an ideal for which I am prepared to die."[30]

His plea fell on unsympathetic ears. On June 12, 1964, he was sentenced to life in prison. From a tiny cell on Robben Island, a popular encampment for political prisoners, Mandela continued to lobby for the emancipation of his brothers and sisters. He used every asset at his disposal, from negotiation to charm. Throughout his years in jail, he attempted to leverage every willing voice outside the walls to help. The years dragged on and the accumulation of his efforts paid off.

In 1989, with world pressure mounting, newly elected South African president F. W. de Klerk began phasing out the policies of apartheid. Finally, on February 12, 1990, Nelson Mandela was released from prison. Four years later, the boy from Mvezo was elected the first black president of South Africa.

LEGACY

As president, Nelson Mandela leaned on the many lessons he learned from his father back at the Great Place at Mqhekezweni, which is African for "a place of learning." Today, tourists flock to the site, now preserved and restored. They can see the school where Mandela studied. They can stand in the church where he came to a personal understanding of Jesus Christ and sang the great hymns of the Christian faith, many of which emphasized emancipation-themed theology. Then there are the buildings which hosted his father and where he was taught servant-style leadership, tolerance, respect, and the art of diplomacy. After being released from prison, Nelson Mandela returned to all of it and reflected on the tremendous influence it had on his life. "There is nothing like returning to a place that remains unchanged to find the ways in which you yourself have altered."[31]

Indeed, many of the same buildings in both of his childhood homes remain unchanged. Villagers continue to wash cups and plates in the same streams he did as a boy nearly a century earlier. Sheep and shepherds still dot the barren countryside, evoking images of times long ago.

But politically, ideologically, and psychologically, everything has changed.

The words of the poet who planted seeds of hope in Mandela's heart came true. And because his adoptive family introduced him to the One who brings ultimate hope and dignity, Nelson Mandela developed the fortitude to press on in the face of adversity without growing bitter.

When the former South African president was laid to rest in his boyhood village of Qunu on December 15, 2013, Monwabisi Jamangile, the chaplain general of the South African military, offered a final and fitting prayer. Facing the flag-draped casket, the pastor said "Now you have achieved ultimate freedom in the bosom of your Maker."[32] A military jet roared overhead and a twenty-one-gun salute echoed across the sky.

Nelson Mandela's long walk to freedom was finally complete.

ADOPTION IN ANCIENT TIMES

Adoption has existed in some fashion since the beginning of human history. Whether motivated or necessitated by death, desire (altruistic or financial), desertion or the incapacitation of one or more birth parents, the transfer of children (or adults) between individuals and families has been an acceptable, albeit exceptional, means of family formation.

Over the years, references to adoption have been recorded in the Bible, numerous historic texts, Greek and Roman mythologies, movies, music, television, and even popular children's literature.

In the Old Testament book of Exodus, we read how the Egyptian King Pharaoh, concerned the Israelites were becoming too numerous and thus a threat to his reign, ordered the area's midwives to kill every newborn male. When a Levite woman named Jochebed gave birth to a baby boy (Moses), she refused to throw the child in the river. Jochebed initially hid him, but later places three-month-old Moses in a basket and sets it amongst the reeds of the Nile River. Pharaoh's daughter finds the baby. Ironically, not knowing who the baby's mother is, she asked Jochebed, his birth mother, to nurse him, which she readily agrees to do (Exodus 2:1–9). Pharaoh's daughter eventually adopts Moses, who grows up to be a prince and one day would dramatically lead the Israelites out of Egypt (Exodus 14).

Esther is another prominent figure in the Bible who was adopted following the death of her parents. Originally named Hadassah, she was taken in by her older cousin, Mordecai, and raised in Persia. After concealing her Jewish faith, she was chosen to be queen to King Xerxes and soon learned of a devious plot to kill the Jews. Queen Esther wants to warn the king, but women (even a queen) can't simply approach royalty without first receiving permission. To do so could cost Esther her life or at least her status and position. What is she to do? She asks her adoptive father for advice.

"Do not think that because you are in the king's house you alone of all the Jews will escape," Mordecai warns. "For if you remain silent at this time, relief and deliverance for the Jews will arise from another place, but you and your father's family will perish. And who knows but that you have come to royal position for such a time as this?" (Esther 4:13–14). King Xeres was grateful for the intelligence. He ordered the plotter, Hamam the Agagite, to be hanged. Mordecai was rewarded by being appointed prime minister.

ANCIENT ROME

In ancient Rome, the typical adoptee wasn't a child but instead a male adult. Families with wealth, power, and social responsibility who lacked a male heir to whom to entrust their inheritance and/or political position and succession would search for an appropriate person, usually someone outside the family blood lines. Significant sums of money were often exchanged along with rights to the individual.

Augustus, the first emperor of the Roman Empire, was born Gaius Octavian. It was his great uncle, Julius Caesar, who named him to be his heir prior to being assassinated in 44 B.C. Many of the Empire's leaders were likewise "adopted," including Tiberius, Caligula, Nero, and Marcus Aurelius.

ANCIENT GREECE

Athenian law was similar to Roman law. There were three types of adoptions in ancient Greece. All were motivated by a desire to provide for family caretaking as generations would live together and thus need assistance as the patriarch of the clan grew older. The first type was called "Inter Vivos," or an adoption during the individual's lifetime. The second was known as "Testamentary," which was adoption decreed within a person's will. Adoptions were also allowed to be executed posthumously, or after the parent had died, even if their will didn't specify any particular arrangement.

Regardless of the specific motivating factor, adoptions have always sought to grant the adoptee the same rights and privileges they would have had as biological heirs of the adopter.

CHAPTER FOUR

BABE RUTH

B y the time he retired from baseball in 1935, George Herman Ruth Jr., otherwise known as Babe Ruth, was probably the most famous and beloved athlete the world had ever seen.

"If Babe Ruth had not existed," said the popular and prolific baseball writer Donald Honig, "it would have been impossible to have invented him. He was the Fourth of July, a brass band and New Year's Eve all rolled into one."[1]

But if not for the love, care, guidance, and influence of a Canadian priest living in Baltimore, Maryland, Ruth's future would have certainly looked very different.

His name was Matthias Leo Boutilier, an imposing 6'5" Xaverian Brother from St. Mary's Industrial School for Boys, a Catholic orphanage and reformatory for "incorrigible" youth that first opened in 1866. Brother Matthias, as he was known, was the main disciplinarian at the school. He also served as its athletic director. Blond haired and blue eyed, the burly Boutilier was constantly breaking up fights and dishing out punishments. He was tough, but he was also fair.

Most importantly, though, he served as a surrogate parent to many of the orphaned boys, who like Ruth, were struggling with the absence of a male role model. It would be impossible to overstate his influence on the future Hall of Famer.

"It was at St. Mary's that I met and learned to love the greatest man I've ever known," wrote Ruth of his hero, Brother Matthias, in his autobiography. "He was the father I needed. He taught me to read and write, and the difference between right and wrong."[2]

George Herman Ruth spent the vast majority of his early life (twelve years) at St. Mary's, and though he was never formally adopted by the Catholic prelate, the relationship along with the tenure of the arrangement has forever placed Babe Ruth in the pantheon of the adopted.

A TOUGH BEGINNING

At the time of his birth on February 6, 1895, George's mother, a German immigrant named Catherine "Katie" Schaumberger, was just twenty years old. She was a diminutive woman at just four feet, ten inches tall. Babe's father, George Ruth, was twenty-three. George Jr. was their first of eight children, though six of them, including twins, died in infancy. Only George Jr. and his sister, Mary, known as Mamie, survived.

According to Ruth biographer Leigh Montville:

> There are no stories of a mother, none, good or bad or madhouse crazy. There is one picture of her, a grainy shot, pulled from a group photo of a family reunion, her famous child on her lap. Her hair is up. Her high collar is buttoned. She is not smiling.
>
> There are few stories of a father. He was a lightning-rod salesman and the owner of a succession of taverns. He had an anger that coursed through him. Or so it seemed.[3]

Why is so little known of Babe Ruth's biological family? Quite simply, it's because he and his sister, who died in 1992 at the age of ninety-one, either didn't know much or decided not to tell what little they did. Curiously, much of what they did share wasn't accurate. For example, Babe Ruth once said he had an older brother named John who died in a street fight. Mamie insisted George was the oldest. Birth and death certificates confirm she was right. The Babe also contended their mother was a mixture of Irish and English descent. Mamie said she was German. Records would seem to confirm her side of the story. After George came John, then twin boys, Joseph and William, and girls, Katherine, Annie, Elizabeth, and Mary (Mamie).

What we do know is the family was poor and ran with a tough and rowdy crowd. Babe Ruth was born at 216 Emory Street in Baltimore, the home of his maternal grandmother. The neighborhood was known as Pigtown, which got its names because of the pigs that ran from the area's stockyard to the slaughterhouse. Hungry residents were known to try and grab them as they ran wildly through the streets and illegally butcher their catch themselves.

DECISION POINT

Over one hundred years later, nobody knows for certain why George's father decided to drop him off at St. Mary's on June 13, 1902. His father wept. The official legal form that his parents signed along with a Justice of the Peace listed the seven-year-old as "incorrigible and vicious" and "beyond the control" of his parents. When asked about it years later, the Babe would simply say his parents entrusted him to the care of St. Mary's because he was "a bad kid." But how bad can a seven-year-old be? What did he actually do? Or perhaps, what didn't he do?

According to biographer Marshall Smelser, prior to enrolling in St. Mary's, a young Ruth "was left alone to run the streets and piers where he trained strenuously to be the champion of truancy…"[4] We know from Ruth and many of those closest to him he despised the classroom and often refused to attend. "He would not go to school," said his sister

Mamie. "And they (their parents) did not have the time to look after him as they should."[5] Is it coincidental or instructive that the same year George was dropped off at St. Mary's the Maryland legislature made school attendance mandatory for all children between the ages of eight and twelve? It's impossible to know.

As an adult, Ruth once told the story of stealing a dollar from his father's cash register in the bar and using it to buy ice cream for every kid on the block. His father horsewhipped him for the offense. When George defied his father and stole from him again, the decision was made to make the sad trip to the imposing institution on Caton and Wilkens Avenues.

RHYTHM AND ROUTINE

At St. Mary's, George finally found what every child intuitively and instinctively wants—order and predictability. The Xaverian brothers who ran the school were not drill sergeants, but they demanded and commanded respect from the boys. They received it. But loving, leading, and managing them was no easy task for even the most experienced teacher. Each grade was comprised of boys from three different groups. First there were orphans, like George, whose biological parents had either died or relinquished control of them. Then there were juvenile delinquents who ran afoul of the law and were sent to the school for the purposes of rehabilitation. Finally, there were boys whose mothers and fathers simply wanted to enroll them in a religious boarding school, primarily for academic or spiritual reasons. All three groups were comingled and for the most part, they all got along with the exception of an occasional fight.

Some have speculated that one of the reasons for the peaceful integration was that school officials never blamed the boys for their circumstances that brought them there. Instead they cited the inadequate care they received at home. The brothers of St. Mary's would be their new family and through thick or thin, they were committed to helping them succeed in life on an emotional, spiritual, and physical level.

When the school was founded by Archbishop Martin J. Spalding, the over-arching goal was to provide a rigorous environment for the development of a well-balanced boy. He wanted the boys to graduate from the school with both head knowledge and practical, employable skills. He encouraged administrators to see each of the students as unique creations who required personalized care and assessment. Without saying as much, he was acknowledging the fact "one-size-fits-all" schools invariably and inevitably shortchange students, often treating them as just another cog in the wheel. Instead, it's the wise teacher who watches them and identifies their special talents, encouraging them to purposefully pursue a field of endeavor best suited to their strengths.

Coming from a chaotic and unstructured home life, George's introduction to St. Mary's was a culture shock. But, he was still young and impressionable and had little trouble adjusting. He found himself attending academic classes in writing, reading, and handwriting for five hours each day. Although never known for his academic prowess later in life, his sparkling and elegant penmanship was the product of years of dedicated instruction and hard work. Biographer Leigh Montville wrote that Ruth "would write with his right hand, not his natural left, in an elegant script that was fashioned by assorted whacks on his wrist by a brother's wooden ruler."[6]

Forcing a naturally left-handed student to write with their right hand was a common characteristic of Catholic education in the twentieth century. Another four hours of each day was spent in shop class. The boys had their choice of training to be a printer, banker, brush maker, bookbinder, shoemaker, carpenter, electrician, millwright, farmer, electrician, knitter, or shirt maker. George chose to be a shirt maker and became so proficient in the trade that he used to brag he could make a shirt in less than fifteen minutes. Inside the Industrial Arts building, which still stands today, the youngster honed his craft, assuming he would likely make his living as a tailor. Even when he was the wealthiest ballplayer in the major leagues, Ruth continued to sew his own shirts.

A SPIRITUAL AWAKENING

Being a Catholic school, students were required to attend daily Mass in the chapel followed by thirty minutes of religious instruction. For

Ruth, the spiritual influence of the many brothers, especially Brother Matthias, was profound. "Up till then (attending St. Mary's), like all bad kids," Ruth once wrote, "I hated most of the people who had control over me and could punish me. [But thanks to the brothers] I began to see that I had a higher Person to reckon with who never changed, whereas my earthly authorities changed from year to year. I also realized that God was not only just, but merciful. He knew we were weak and that we all found it easier to be stinkers than good sons of God, not only as kids but all through our lives."[7]

What Ruth was getting at, albeit in a more colorful way, was the fact a child's first impression of God is so often shaped by the relationship they have with a mother, father, or other authoritative figure. Psychologists will tell you if the guardian of a child is kind, gentle, and just, the child will often see God in similar fashion. However, if the individual is impatient, cutting, and downright mean, that same child will assume God is likewise spiteful, vengeful, and not to be trusted.

In the brothers of St. Mary's, George found a responsible and noble representation of the sacred. He also developed an enormous spirit of compassion, especially for children. Ruth's visits to hospitals to cheer up sick youngsters have become legendary. He also found it impossible to say no to almost any charitable request and would spend hours signing autographs and regaling those gathered with humorous stories. In many ways, he was ministering out of his own deficits and had a keen understanding of what it was like to be poor and in search of love and acceptance.

A STAR IS BORN

At St. Mary's, athletics was another significant outlet for the boys, and all of them were encouraged to participate. According to school records, with nearly one thousand students on campus, there were twenty-eight uniformed teams to play on throughout the course of the year. There was football, soccer, wrestling, boxing, swimming, and of course, baseball. But baseball, as it was across the nation, was dominant. Various leagues were established based on ability, and the students played one another on the diamond between the buildings. Brother Paul Scanlon, the superintendent of the school who was also technically George's legal guardian, saw sports as more than mere fun, but rather a requirement of a well-balanced life. "Play activities [are] an eighth sacrament without which it would practically be impossible to have a sound mind," he once said.[8]

There are various accounts of how George gravitated to baseball over all the other sports at the school. One suggests he was already familiar with the game and had played in the streets prior to arriving. Another credits one of the brothers with asking him what position he played and then tossing him a left-handed catcher's mitt, and George putting it on the wrong hand. What we do know is on Saturday nights after supper, Brother Matthias hit "fungos" (high fly balls with a thin bat) to the boys in the yard. More than five hundred would convene to shag the balls, George among them.

George was particularly intrigued with Matthias's dramatic, upward cut. At the time, most major league ballplayers swung downward in a chopping motion, and so this change was exciting for the impressionable boy. "I'll never forget the first time I saw him hit a ball," said Ruth. "The baseball in 1902 was a lump of mush, but Brother Matthias would stand at the end of the yard, throw the ball up with his left hand, and give it a terrific belt with the bat he held in his right hand. The ball would carry 350 feet, a tremendous knock in those days. I would watch him bug-eyed."[9]

George noticed the imposing prelate also ran with short "pigeon-toed" steps believing it to be more efficient. "He used to back me in a corner of the big yard at St. Mary's and bunt a ball to me by the hour," Ruth remembered, "correcting the mistakes I made with my hands and feet."[10] The young Ruth worked hard to emulate both the swing and the stride, two characteristics that would ultimately define the rising star.

According to the biographer Leigh Montville, "Brother Matthias was an accessible hero" to Ruth.[11]

It wasn't long before George became known as the most talented ballplayer in the school. Playing in as many as two hundred games a year,

Ruth had plenty of opportunity to develop his talent. He loved catching since it allowed him to be in the middle of every play, although with only a catcher's mitt for a righty, he had to improvise. Catching the ball with his left hand, George would quickly switch the ball to his right hand, toss the glove in the air and then transfer the ball back to his left in order to throw. When Ruth criticized the quality of the team's pitching, Brother Matthias called his bluff, challenging him to try and do better.

"If you know so much about pitching," Matthias cracked, "why not do it yourself?"[12]

He did and quickly developed a reputation as a star pitcher.

He was impossible to miss on the field or off. "He was pretty big for his age," said Brother Herman, one of the many priests of St. Mary's. "Not flashy, in fact more on the wiry side, he was still an outstanding looking boy. He had a mop of thick dark-brown hair. He was livelier than most of the boys, full of mischief. There was nothing timid about him. He was an aggressive, shouting boy who was always wrestling around with the others. He held his own, too."[13]

ON HIS WAY

From age eight to eighteen, Ruth lived under the care and guidance of St. Mary's. There are indications his mother came to visit him from time to time, but never his father. After his mother died in 1912, likely of tuberculosis, not a single person came to see him. Louis "Fats" Leisman, a classmate, recalls Ruth telling him, half-jokingly, "Well, I guess I am too big and ugly for anyone to come to see me. Maybe next time." Leisman concluded, "But next time never came."[14]

George's big break came in February of 1914 when Brother Gilbert reached out to a friend and baseball scout for the Baltimore Orioles, Jack Dunn. Intrigued by the ringing endorsement, a scrappy baseball man who made a career of discovering talented players in the most unlikely places came to St. Mary's for a visit. Brothers Matthias and Gilbert escorted him around campus in search of the prospect. They found Ruth in a pair of overalls outside the shirt shop, chewing on tobacco and horsing around with his classmates. From the scouting report, Dunn was aware Ruth could hit.

"Can he pitch?" he asked.

"Sure," Brother Matthias answered. "He can do anything."

After observing Ruth in action, Jack Dunn offered the eighteen-year-old a contract for $250 month. The idea of getting paid to play baseball almost seemed too good to be true. But it wasn't. It was really happening. Still technically under the guardianship of Brother Paul, Ruth received his and Matthias's blessing. He excitedly signed the contract and spent part of his first paycheck on a bicycle. Arriving in spring training in North Carolina, veteran players were told to go easy on one of Jack's "babes." His youthful and pudgy face added credibility to the moniker. At first considered something of a joke, the nickname stuck.

George "Babe" Herman Ruth was on his way to a prolific big league journey that would eventually propel him to near mythical worldwide status. After just five months in Baltimore, he was sold to the Boston Red Sox and in December of 1919, he was traded to the New York Yankees. Playing in New York in the aftermath of the cheating scandal in Chicago, Ruth was just what baseball needed as it worked to repair its image. Here was a man people could pull for—a big-hearted young man with a smile and a swing that sent balls out of ballparks at a record rate. In his first year with the Yankees he hit fifty-four home runs—more than any other team combined. In 1921, he whacked fifty-nine. People flocked from all over to see him. "The name helped," remarked biographer Robert Creamer. "If his name was Harold Thompson, I don't think it would have had the same impact."[15]

In 1936, Babe Ruth's legendary career landed him into the very first class of the National Baseball Hall of Fame.

LASTING INFLUENCE

His on-field exploits well-established, part of Ruth's charm and fame also stemmed, as previously noted, from his reputation as one of the game's most charitable and generous players. Yet, Ruth's spiritual and personal journey was something of a paradox. "I like to live as big as I can," he once said—and he meant every word of it.[16] He ate and drank too much. He was also sexually promiscuous and separated from his first wife, Helen Woodford, due to reported infidelities. Yet, after a night of carousing, he'd drag his teammates out of bed in order to attend morning Mass. After a recitation of the Rosary, all was right—until he did it all over again the next night.

Reflecting on his past, Ruth once admitted with regret, "Out on my own, free from the rigid rules of a religious school…boy did it go to my head. I began really to cut capers."[17] But it was the lasting influence of Brother Matthias and the moral and spiritual foundation that was laid at St. Mary's that eventually brought him back. "I doubt if any appeal could have straightened me out except a Power over and above man—the appeal of God," he wrote just days before his death in 1948 and later published in *Guideposts Magazine*.[18] "Iron-rod discipline couldn't have done it. Nor all the punishment and reward systems that could have been devised. God had an eye out for me, just as He has for you, and He was pulling for me to make the grade."[19]

His voice only a whisper as he lay dying of throat cancer, Ruth's final words continued in the folksy manner he was known for:

"The lads who get religious training, get it where it counts—in the roots. They may fail it, but it never fails them. When the score is against them, or they get a bum pitch, that unfailing Something inside will be there to draw on. I've seen it with kids. I know from the letters they wrote me. The more I think of it, the more important I feel it is to give kids 'the works' as far as religion is concerned. They'll never want to be holy—they'll act like tough monkeys in contrast, but somewhere inside will be a solid little chapel. It may get dusty from neglect, but the time will come when the door will be opened with much relief. But the kids can't take it, if we don't give it to them."[20]

The focal point of Ruth's last essay was children, but according to those closest to him, Ruth, perhaps unconsciously, always saw himself as a young boy of Baltimore, still scrapping, climbing, and dreaming. According to his old teacher, Brother Gilbert, Ruth was "free from guile and deceit of any kind. He had implicit faith in the whole world; and he looked out on that world with the grave and solemn wonder of a child."[21]

On August 19, 1948, with close to six thousand people attending his funeral inside and seventy-five thousand waiting outside in the rain at New York City's St. Patrick's Cathedral, George Herman Ruth was laid to rest. Inside his closed casket, in his now still, cold left hand, the same hand that enabled him to ascend to the heights of fame and fortune as well as struggle with all the sins of a fallen world, was placed a baseball with the following three word inscription:

Safe at Home

He was just fifty-three years old.

CHAPTER FIVE

JOHN HANCOCK

Why is it that so many know so little about the man with the most famous signature in American history?

If you ask the average person about John Hancock, you're likely to hear them talk about his elegant penmanship and how he boldly signed the Declaration of Independence on July 4, 1776, placing his name in the center of the historic document. In fact, many attribute his motivation for inscribing so prominently and disproportionately in size to the others as an act of indignation and defiance to Great Britain.

"There," he's purported to have said upon signing. "I guess King George will be able to read that without his spectacles!"[1]

As the president of the Continental Congress in 1776, John Hancock was, indeed, the first colonist to affix his signature to the parchment. As for the size of his name and the motivation behind it and its placement—such is the substance of myth and legend. Although he did reportedly exclaim upon signing, "The British ministry can read that name without spectacles; let them double their reward," the document was addressed to neither King George III nor the British Parliament.[2] To do so, the colonists feared, would have further legitimized an unresponsive and dictatorial regime. Instead, the document was primarily drafted as a means by which to communicate with colonial legislatures.

Handwriting analysts have long attempted to decipher the signature and draw conclusions about the man behind it. They suggest its size indicates a spirit of self-importance, the ornateness an ostentatious attitude, and its overall boldness a flair for the dramatic.

Are they accurate?

Biographer Herbert S. Allen described John Hancock as something of a contradiction, though very human, to be sure. Allen called Hancock "the most neglected and maligned of famous figures in the annals of America," suggesting he was a "tactful and adept mediator, an intelligent compromiser, a true patriot, and a generous and sympathetic lover of the common people."[3] Yet, at the same time, Allen said he was simultaneously "vain, petty and pompous...an exasperating man."[4]

All of which makes him a wonderfully rich and colorful figure to study.

HUMBLE BEGINNINGS

When John Hancock was born on January 23, 1737, to the Reverend John Hancock Jr. and Mary Hawk Thaxter, the family's rural home in Braintree (modern day Quincy), Massachusetts, was just ten miles south of Boston. Yet compared with the bustling environment of the "big city" in pace and lifestyle, it may just as well have been hundreds of miles away. John was the second born of three children. Mary was two years older and his younger brother Ebenezer arrived in 1741.

John's father, the Reverend Hancock, served as pastor of the United First Parish Church, a Puritan Congregationalist body that would later become affiliated with the Unitarian denomination. The Reverend Hancock's father and John Hancock's grandfather was the Reverend John Hancock Sr., a highly revered clergyman who pastored in Lexington. His congregation called him "Bishop" although it wasn't an official title.

He served as pastor for fifty-four years until his death in 1752. The Reverend Hancock counted amongst his peers the lions of the Great Awakening, including George Whitefield and Jonathan Edwards.

Back in Braintree, the younger Hancock's congregation claimed as its members the future president John Adams and years later, the Adams' son and the sixth president, John Quincy. The Reverend Hancock actually baptized John Adams as a child and, of course, his own son, John III. Subsisting on the meager provisions of a pastor's salary, the family lived modestly in a manse provided by the church. On the adjacent land they grew vegetables and raised pigs and cattle.

In Colonial America, towns normally formed official schools if they had fifty or more families. Braintree had far fewer, and so the children of the hamlet relied on either traditional homeschooling or what was then called "Dame Schools"—an early form of private education featuring a local woman as the teacher. In 1742, five-year-old John Hancock joined seven-year-old John Adams at Mrs. Belcher's country homeschool. At the time, it was understood John would follow in the footsteps of his father and enter the ministry after college. The idea appealed to the young boy, who really knew nothing else. Life was placid, calm, and predictable, even idyllic. But circumstances were about to change significantly and with it, the destiny of John Hancock III.

A TRAGIC TURN OF THE TIDE

In 1744, John's father, the Reverend John Hancock II, was forty-two years of age and in the midst of his eighteenth year as pastor of United First Parish Church. He was well-loved and a highly respected figure in the town of Braintree. According to a contemporary, "His prayers and sermons were judiciously composed and gravely uttered in the language of the Holy Scripture."[5] As a man, he was described as being "faithful and prudent...meek and humble...[and a] bright and engaging example" to his flock.[6] Content and still challenged and still with a nine-, seven-, and three-year-old toddling around the manse, he had no plans to go anywhere, especially since his own father was still pastoring in

Lexington. But then sickness came and the once vibrant preacher was soon confined to his bed. He died on Monday, May 7, 1744.

At his funeral later that week, with his wife and three children huddled together in the front pew, a friend and fellow pastor, Ebenezer Gay of Braintree's First Church of Christ, preached the sermon, stressing the importance of embracing the sovereignty of God in times of sorrow. "Untimely death is an event that happens to both the righteous and to the wicked," he said. "In God's hand is the breath of all mankind."[7] He went on to praise his late friend for enduring his illness with "admirable patience" and concluded with a tribute and charge to the assembled: "How great a help and comfort … how sweet to us has been his conversation … how sound his advice … how tender his sympathy with us in our troubles. Our strength is now weakened. His end is peace…Let us all be excited to follow him, as he followed Christ."[8]

Because the family's home had been provided by the church, the widow Mary was now left to find alternative housing for her young family. Seven-year-old John was taken to his grandfather's in Lexington. It was assumed the Bishop could raise him there, ensuring his eventual path toward ordination. What the boy thought of all this is unclear, but with his world now turned upside down, Johnny simply went where he was told to go.

BOSTON BOUND

Meanwhile up in Boston, Thomas Hancock, a son of the Bishop and John's uncle, was thriving as the owner and proprietor of the "House of Hancock," a Boston mercantile business that regularly traded with Newfoundland, Spain, and Portugal. Thomas got his start at the age of thirteen, working an apprenticeship with a Boston bookbinder and bookseller. In 1723 he opened his own bookshop and a year later launched the mercantile. By 1744, Thomas was forty-one years of age and he and his wife, Lydia, had no children of their own. Concerned for his nephew and searching for an heir to one day take over the family business, Thomas offered to adopt John. He promised to send John to Harvard, a Hancock tradition, and also agreed to financially support his sister-in-law and her two remaining children. Everyone was in agreement.

For John, the transition from the rural life in Braintree and the quiet life as a pastor's son to the opulent house on Beacon Hill and a world of global trade and high society was dramatic. Conversely, the childless couple were ecstatic to welcome a youngster into their midst. Arriving from Lexington, the youngster stepped into what was arguably the grandest home in all of Boston. The Hancocks lived in a two-story house made of granite, fifty-three feet wide by sixty-three feet deep with fifty-four windows (each with a lit candle at night). It was every bit a mansion, and something straight from the pages of a fairy tale. Only it was a real place, and his aunt and uncle, now his adopted mother and father, were not wicked step-parents, but instead loving and doting parents who promised to treat him as if he were one of their own.

ADJUSTING TO LIFE ON BEACON HILL

Sensitive to the grief and natural adjustments required of their newly adopted son, Thomas and Lydia decided to homeschool John for the first year, a decision that proved wise. He slipped seamlessly into city life, comfortably and eagerly donning and subscribing to the fashions of the day. Around town he was often seen wearing velvet britches, lace trimmed shirts, and leather shoes with silver buckles. In July of 1745, his parents enrolled him in the Public Latin School, the first public institution in America. Today it remains the oldest existing school in the United States.

In 1745, students desiring admittance to elementary school were required to be able to read several passage of the Bible. From there, though, expectations skyrocketed. By the completion of his first year, ten-year-old John was required to have read and mastered Cheever's *Accidence*, *Nomenclatura Brevis*, and Corderius's *Colloquies* (in Latin). By the end of year four, a student was expected to be able to write in Latin. The former farm boy showed no signs of difficulty keeping up with the rigors of his classes.

HARVARD MAN

At the age of thirteen, John sat for entrance examinations for Harvard. The decision helped his adoptive father fulfill a promise he made to John's biological mother and grandfather just six years earlier. In 1750, entrance exams were given orally with the exception of having to create and produce an essay written in Latin. According to the printed instructions, John would be required "extempore to read, construe, and parse Tully, Virgil, or such like common classical Latin authors; and...ordinary Greek, as in the New Testament; Isocrates, or such like, and decline the paradigms of Greek nouns and verbs."[9]

John passed with flying colors and began attending classes in August of 1750. Student life in Cambridge was rigorous and regimented. Students were required to attend daily chapel at six o'clock in the morning, followed by a Scripture reading study in Hebrew or Greek, followed by breakfast. Classwork followed. The evening meal, which was always taken together as a group, included a half-pint of beer, which the teenage Hancock heartily consumed. As a student, John was considered "simply a respectable, good-mannered lad, obedient to his supervisors, and a faithful student in school."[10]

Graduating with a Master of Arts degree on July 17, 1754, at the age of seventeen, John assumed a full-time role as clerk as part of an apprenticeship with his father at the House of Hancock.

THE MERCHANT PRINCE

Outside the classroom, John's new father tutored him in the family business. Thomas Hancock also trained him in the fine art of conversation and socialization. In order for a merchant to be successful, he asserted, one needed to know not only how to get along with people but also how to negotiate and persuade them to your point of view. John spent countless hours at long lunches that turned into late evening meetings. Those who knew both men would say John's manners were "very gracious" and clearly "of the old school" and "dignified."[11]

Following the arrival of John, business at the House of Hancock continued to thrive, though the French and Indian War complicated and impacted shipping routes and thus, access to products. But they managed, and by 1760, Thomas decided it was time to send his son to England to further his education in the business. The two-year trip was deemed a success, though John appeared to regularly frustrate his parents with his infrequent communications.

FROM LOSS TO LEADERSHIP

Thomas Hancock's health began failing during the summer of 1764. He died of a stroke on August 1st. John's apprenticeship at the House of Hancock was officially over. As expected, the twenty-three-year-old inherited his father's estate, which was estimated to be worth millions in today's dollars. Overnight he became one of the wealthiest men in Boston and assumed full control of the family business. John slid comfortably into the role, regularly entertaining at the Hancock mansion on Beacon Hill.

By the middle of the 1760s, colonists were growing increasingly frustrated with the onerous taxes Great Britain was charging on trade, most notably the Stamp and Townsend Acts. As the head of a business dedicated to trade, John was particularly agitated at what many deemed to be "taxation without representation"—the new rallying cry of the colonies.

Hancock was eager for change, but was initially cool to the idea of aggressive action, which several of his friends advocated. He was already active in the political circles of Boston, recently joining the Long Room Club with friends such as Paul Revere, Thomas Dawes, Dr. Benjamin Church, and the Reverend Samuel Cooper. They met in a room above the *Boston Gazette*, which gladly cooperated in helping to galvanize support for a rebellion through its reporting and editorials. As time progressed, Samuel Adams and others pleaded with Hancock to act. With his wealth and status, they contended, a move by Hancock could help trigger the revolution they felt was needed.

After a series of scuffles with inspectors examining several of Hancock's shipments in the spring of 1768, John Hancock reached his limit.

At one point, he and his people trapped a British customs official, nailing shut a door so they could unload the vast majority of the goods, thus reducing their tax burden. After openly refusing to pay tariffs on goods from shipments, including a cargo load of his favorite Madeira wine on the *Liberty* (how ironic!), British officials seized control of the ship's contents and accused him of smuggling. As biographer Herbert S. Allen rightly observed, "Hancock now enjoyed the paradoxical position of having gained immeasurably by the loss of the *Liberty*. His popularity heretofore had been based chiefly on kindheartedness. Henceforth it was to have the additional prop of stout-heartedness."[12]

The seizure electrified the budding revolutionaries in Boston. Violence erupted throughout the city. British troops were brought in, further enraging the colonists. Following the Boston Massacre on March 5, 1770, John Hancock accused British officials of "trampling on the rights and liberties of his most loyal subjects."[13]

The American Revolution was well underway with John Hancock helping to lead the fight.

PUBLIC SERVANT

Both John Hancock and John Adams, thanks to the famous midnight ride of Paul Revere, narrowly escaped British capture in April of 1775. From Lexington, Hancock traveled to Philadelphia and was elected president of the Second Continental Congress. In May he married Dorothy Quincy. (Sadly, their two children, Lydia and John, did not make it out of childhood.) In 1778, Hancock was appointed Major General of the Massachusetts Militia, and in 1780 he was elected governor of Massachusetts, where he served five consecutive one-year terms until poor health forced him to step down in 1785. He was elected again to the post in 1787 and served as governor until his death in 1793. Although General George Washington ran for the most part unopposed for president in 1789, Hancock expressed interest in the office. He was disappointed when John Adams was elected vice president, a role he also wanted.

At what would be his last public appearance on September 18, 1793, testifying before the legislature at a special session he called to discuss the sovereignty of the state, Hancock's speech was read by the Secretary of State. Then, struggling to stand, Hancock personally addressed those in attendance. "I feel the seeds of mortality growing fast within me," he said. "But I think I have, in this case, done no more than my duty as the servant of the people. I never did, and I never will, deceive them while I have life and strength to act in their service."[14]

Just three weeks later on October 8, 1793, Hancock died of gout and exhaustion, "resigning his soul into the hands of Him who gave it."[15] He was just fifty-six years old.

LEGACY

That a boy who had experienced such domestic strife could grow up to become one of the wealthiest men in Boston, help lead a revolution, and serve nearly ten terms as governor is not only one of the great stories of American history, but also of the institution and power of adoption. From helping him find his true calling to helping the colonists find their voice and inspiration for changing the status quo, Thomas and Lydia's decision to welcome seven-year-old John into their home should not just be a footnote in history, but a headline. After all, later in life, it was Hancock's willingness to risk his family's fortune for the sake of independence that helped trigger the birth of a new nation.

And it might never have happened had John Hancock not been adopted.

According to John Adams, "He [Hancock] inherited from his [adoptive] father, though one of the most amiable and beloved of men, a certain sensibility, a keenness of feeling, or, in more familiar language, a peevishness of temper, that sometimes disgusted and afflicted his friends. Yet it was astonishing with what patience, perseverance, and punctuality, he attended to business to the last. Nor were his talents or attainments inconsiderable. They were far superior to many who have been much more celebrated. He had a great deal of political sagacity and penetration into men."[16]

In Boston on Monday, October 14, 1793, drums rattled and cannons boomed. John Hancock was laid to rest beside his adoptive father, Thomas Hancock. Over twenty thousand participated in the procession, the largest funeral the country had ever seen.

CHAPTER SIX

DAVE THOMAS

Rex David Thomas was born in Atlantic City, New Jersey, on July 2, 1932, the same day the future four-term President Franklin Delano Roosevelt accepted the Democratic nomination. In his address from the convention stage inside Chicago Stadium, the charismatic Roosevelt observed that the two things Americans wanted more than anything else were "work and security"—two items in desperately short supply in the depth of the ongoing Great Depression.[1]

Ironically or perhaps fortuitously, it would be the absence of both of these virtues in Thomas's early life—and their presence in the latter— that would mark, measure, and define his life and career.

MYSTERY

What is known about the details surrounding Dave Thomas's birth? Not all that much. We know his birth mother was a young, unmarried woman named Mollie. She was from Camden, New Jersey, a bustling port town just north of Philadelphia. In 1932, Camden was a city of thirty thousand and housed three major companies: the New York Ship-building Corporation, RCA, and Campbell's Soup. Mollie's parents owned a tailor shop there and likely served men and women from those three businesses. We know at the time of Dave's arrival, she was not dating his birthfather. He was named Sam. From the archives of the local paper we know the particular Saturday of his birth was sunny with a high of eighty degrees, a bit cool for swimming but ideal for a stroll along the iconic boardwalk of the seaside city.

Had his biological parents met at the beach the previous summer? Perhaps, but it's impossible to know. All Dave would later say is she was "in trouble" but didn't know what kind, though presumably it had to do with the embarrassment of conceiving a child out of wedlock.[2] We do know in the months leading up to the birth of the only child she would ever bear, Mollie made the short trip from Camden to Atlantic City and checked into a home for unwed mothers. She gave birth at a hospital there, not far from the boardwalk, kissed her one and only son, entrusted him to the care of the home and returned, almost certainly in tears, to Camden and life in the family shop.

When Dave was twenty-one, he decided to try and find Mollie. He was curious, and like most adoptees of that era, he had lots of questions. The records were sealed. By 1953, after doing some searching on his own, he found the family's tailor shop. Sadly, he discovered Mollie had died years earlier of rheumatic fever. He felt no emotional connection to her family and so he politely thanked them and moved on. Since no one seemed to know anything about his biological father, Thomas decided to forgo any further investigation.

It wasn't until the mid-1980s, with his permission, that one of his own daughters, hoping to find some family health history, located one of Sam's cousins. His biological father was no longer living. Dave discovered he had a half-brother, a college professor. But the gentleman flat-out refused to meet, fearing his mother would be upset to learn her husband fathered another child, adding he didn't know if his father was even aware of Dave.

"He [the half-brother] might be very, very smart," said Dave in retrospect, "but he doesn't have much common sense."[3]

MICHIGAN

Rex and Auleva Thomas arrived from Kalamazoo, Michigan, in August to officially adopt their six-week-old son from the Atlantic City home for unwed mothers. As a child, Rex worked in the oil fields. Now, at twenty-seven, he was a construction foreman. Unable to conceive children naturally, the couple was ecstatic about the adoption. Auleva planned to fulfill her dream of being a full-time mother and homemaker. Rex headed back to work, a proud first-time father. Setting up the nursery back in Kalamazoo, the future for the young family of three seemed bright, even limitless.

TRAGEDY STRIKES

Prior to the widespread availability of penicillin in the late 1940s, the scourge of rheumatic fever—an inflammatory infection affecting the joints, heart, skin, and brain—was raging at epidemic levels. In the 1920s, it was the leading cause of death for those between the ages of five and twenty and the second leading cause of death for those between the ages of twenty to thirty, surpassed only by tuberculosis.[4] To give you an idea of how dangerous the infection was, records indicate that in 1938, eight thousand people died of rheumatic fever in New York City alone. Tragically, its impact was similarly felt in Kalamazoo.[5]

In the fall of 1937, just months past Dave's fifth birthday, Auleva fell victim to the fever. For weeks she lay bedridden until finally succumbing. "I really don't remember her, what she looked like or how she treated me," he said. "But I do remember when she was really sick, and when she died. No one really explained anything, but I remember the smell of her hospital room and how white everything was: her face, the sheets, the floor, the nurses."[6]

Understandably, the trauma on his young senses was profound. "The whole thing was like a strange dream to me," he said. "I didn't know people were supposed to die, and I didn't know who would replace her."[7]

Within five years, although he was then unaware his birth mother died, Dave Thomas lost both mothers to the same illness.

And so, the fairy tale, if it was ever imagined in the first place, was over. There would be no happy ending. The young couple's dream of happily ever after with a child of their own became a tragic nightmare for the thirty-two-year-old widower left behind. His wife and Dave's adoptive mother was gone, and the young boy was faced with a major adjustment.

In a twist only God can turn, it would be an adjustment that planted the seeds for a young boy's dream that eventually came true.

FATHER AND SON

Without Auleva's tender and nurturing temperament in the home, Dave found Rex difficult to navigate. The relationship struggled. His dad was quiet and reserved, a man of few words. Since nobody was home to cook, father and son regularly went out to eat at inexpensive greasy spoons in the neighborhood. One of their favorites was Kewpee's at the corner of Burdick and South in Kalamazoo. Owned and operated by the Weston family since 1923 (and still in operation) the menu consisted of square hamburgers and thick malt shakes.

There they would sit and eat. And since Rex wasn't much of a conversationalist, Dave began to silently study the manager, cashiers, and cooks behind the counter. "I remember watching families sitting together and having a good time," he said. "To me, eating out wasn't just about the food. It was a special event."[8]

To compound the grief and the cold shoulder he was feeling, Dave's father remarried within a year of his mother's death. "Outside of Marie's (his stepmother) picking on my table manners, she and my dad would ignore me during the whole meal. Maybe Marie and my dad Rex had their own problems," he acknowledged. "Maybe I had trouble accepting her as my new mother. I don't know, but I was confused."[9] Rex and Marie's marriage ended after just two and half years.

By the time he was eight, he knew what he wanted to do. "Popeye wasn't my hero. Wimpy was, because he loved hamburgers. I just thought restaurants were really neat, exciting places," he said. "I thought if I owned a restaurant, I could eat all I wanted for free. What could be better than that?"[10]

GRANDMA MINNIE

With Dave's father in the construction business and finding it a challenge to land consistent work, the elementary school–aged boy began spending considerable time, especially summers, with his grandmother Minnie.

Minnie Sinclair was Auleva's mother and lived in Augusta, Michigan. "[She] was the strongest influence in my life," he said. His favorite thing to do with her was to eat together on Saturdays at the lunch counter of the local five and dime. "Don't cut corners. Hard work is good for the soul," he remembers her telling him. "It keeps you from feeling sorry for yourself because you don't have the time."[11]

Throughout his childhood, Minnie served as Thomas's one constant and, outside his faith, the sole source of his security. The time she devoted to personal prayer impressed him. She tried to help him make sense of his mother's death, assuring him she was in heaven and he would see her again. Most importantly, it was Dave's grandmother who introduced him to Christianity. Here is how he recalled his baptism:

> When I was eleven years old, my adoptive grandmother Minnie Sinclair took me to Gull Lake to be baptized by immersion. Gull Lake is in western Michigan, near Kalamazoo, where Calvary Church once stood. Gull Lake's deep blue water was surrounded by big beautiful cottages back then. I really felt that I was accepted by God when I was baptized. But what I remember most about my baptism is that my Grandma Minnie took

me there. For her, Christianity meant more than doctrine, which of course is important; it meant working hard in a restaurant, seeing to the lodgers she rented rooms to, tending a big garden and doing the canning, and sloppin' the hogs every morning. At night she'd listen to gospel radio out of Chicago and on Sundays before church we'd listen to shows like the Cato Tabernacle out of Indianapolis. The public praying and singing part of her faith might not have stuck with me all that much, but I got baptized into the roll-up-your-shirtsleeves kind of faith that Grandma Minnie held.[12]

DISCOVERY

Two years later, in the summer of 1945, Dave found out the big secret his parents and grandmother kept from him for the first thirteen years of his life. It was his grandmother Minnie who finally told him.

"When I found out I was [adopted] I didn't want to talk about it," he said. "I was really mad about it…It really hurt that nobody told me before."[13]

In his later years, Dave Thomas spoke strongly about the importance of telling children who were adopted the truth about their story from an early age—even long before they fully understand adoption. "Hiding the truth about adoption in a family," he wrote, "can quietly do its harm to the birth siblings as much as to the adopted ones."[14]

It would be several decades before Dave felt comfortable talking publicly about his past, but when he started, he couldn't stop and spent the rest of his life serving as an advocate for adoption.

"In the late '80s, we were having a meeting, a kind of motivational meeting for our managers, and I went public," he recalled. "I said, 'If I can do it, you can do it. How many people in this room know your mother and father? Raise your hand if you've never seen your biological mother and father.' And I raised my hand. Then one of my managers came up to me and said, 'I'm adopted. Why don't you talk about adoption?'"[15]

In an instant Dave was convicted and began to talk openly about both his adoption and the importance of children growing up in stable, loving homes, both biological and adopted, even testifying before Congress several times over the years. "A family can count on each other, and that's something that can't be bought or sold. All the small stuff is swept aside when an obstacle is faced. It brings out the best of us. That old saying is true, 'We're stronger when we stand together.' I'm very grateful and proud to be part of the Thomas family."[16]

KEEPING BUSY

Over the span of the next few years, his father's search for work forced Dave and his father to relocate to numerous cities. When he turned ten, his father remarried for the third time and moved to Princeton, Indiana. His step sister had a job and contributed to the finances of the family, something he wanted to do as well. With the nation still gripped in the clutches of the Depression, the enterprising youngster was eager to take his grandmother's advice to keep busy and dutifully searched for work himself. He delivered newspapers and groceries, set pins at a local bowling alley and caddied at a country club.

Upon arriving in Knoxville, Tennessee, he was hired to work at a Walgreen's soda fountain, but was quickly fired when the manager discovered he was only twelve, not sixteen. His father came down hard on him. "He told me I would never keep a job, that he would have to support me the rest of my life. From that moment, I was determined to not lose another job. I wanted to prove him wrong."[17]

He quickly found work at the Regas Restaurant, an establishment owned and run by two brothers, Frank and George. One of the brothers told him to "Work as if your job depends on every single customer, every day."[18] Thomas worked there seven days a week.

In 1947, the Thomases relocated again, this time to Fort Wayne, Indiana. The move served as a turning point in the fifteen-year-old's life. He landed a job as a busboy with the Hobby House restaurant chain, a popular establishment advertising "Popular Foods at Popular Prices."

His salary was fifty cents an hour, and after just one week he received a nickel raise. Impressed with his work ethic and attitude, Phillip Clauss, the restaurant's owner, promoted Dave to the kitchen, and he began working as a cook.

At last, the teenager was thriving. He loved his work. So when his father again lost his job and announced they were moving, Dave resisted. He was tired of the nomadic life and weary of living in a crowded trailer. He convinced his father to let him stay behind. After renting a room at the local YMCA, Dave quit high school and began working full-time at Hobby House. Although the work eventually propelled him into his dream profession, he always regretted the decision to leave school early.

As his father packed the car, minus Dave, the time had come to say good-bye. "Someday you'll be proud of me," he said, tears in his eyes and a lump in his throat. "I'm going to have my own restaurant and I'm going to be a success." Rather than throwing his arms around him, Rex replied, "I hope you're right son. Good luck to you."[19]

Looking back on his decision to quit school early, Dave acknowledged his mistake saying, "I was dumb to drop out." In 1993, forty-six years later, Dave tested for and received his G.E.D. certificate. Coconut Creek High School near his home in Fort Lauderdale voted him most likely to succeed.

ARMY LIFE

The isolation of living alone at the Y began to take its toll, and Dave's boss at the Hobby House suggested he live with his sister and husband. And two kids. He agreed. "They were wonderful people," he shared, "and some of my happiest times were spent with them."[20]

In 1950, anticipating he'd be drafted into the Korean War, Dave joined the Army. He signed up for Cook's and Baker's School at Fort Benning, Georgia. His previous restaurant experience impressed his superiors, and in 1951 he was shipped over to Germany where he served as the assistant manager of an enlisted men's club, providing meals for two thousand soldiers each day. At just twenty years old, he was the youngest to ever hold that position. Before being honorably discharged in 1953, Thomas rose to the rank of staff sergeant.

FATE AND FRIED FOOD

Upon arriving back in the United States in late 1953, a civilian once more, Thomas returned to the Hobby House restaurant in Fort Wayne. He was earning $35 a week and was eager to spread his wings. When the Clausses hired a new eighteen-year-old waitress named Lorraine Buskirk, Dave fell madly in love with her, although he almost blew his chance with her by making a poor first impression.

"I was working as a grill man and one day we were so busy I pushed out order after order and kept ringing the bell for her to pick up the food," he recalled. "She wasn't picking up the orders fast enough, in my opinion, so I kept ringing that bell over and over." What did Lorraine think of the hot shot cook? "I was holding two plates in my hands and I told him, 'Would you like me to serve this, or would you like to wear it?'"[21]

Dave and Lorraine began dating and were married one year later. They wound up having five children: Pam, Kenny, Molly, Lori, and Melinda Lou, nicknamed Wendy. It was an eight-year-old freckled Melinda who was the inspiration for the name of the future hamburger empire.

STRUGGLES AT HOME

As a father, he struggled trying to balance the passions of his work with his responsibilities as a husband and father. He often blamed his bad habits on a lack of a good role model growing up. "He was always overtired," says his daughter Pam. "He really didn't know how to treat kids, didn't know how to go to a baseball game. My mom really held it together."[22] When he was home, on Sundays after church, the kids would often find their father asleep on the couch. Prior to his death, his son Ken told *People* magazine, "He doesn't seem to know how to be with us. For him, home is a nice place to visit, but he doesn't want to live there."[23]

The burger millionaire didn't deny it. "How can I explain?" he asked. "I like to be around them, but I couldn't do it too much because it would bother me. We'd bug each other."[24]

Shortly after meeting Lorraine, Dave was promoted to the role of vice president for Hobby House and tasked with launching a new BBQ restaurant called the Hobby Ranch House. In 1956, when the Clauss family entered talks with an eccentric restaurateur named Harland Sanders about buying several of his Kentucky Fried Chicken franchises, Thomas was skeptical.

"Why should we pay some guy who looks like a billy goat 5 cents apiece for chicken when we already have good chicken?" he asked. He later saw its value. "It turned out that his chicken took less time to prepare and customers wanted to see what Kentucky Fried Chicken was all about."[25]

THE FUTURE IS COLUMBUS

After the four KFC franchises the Clauss family purchased in Columbus, Ohio, failed to turn a profit, they approached Dave with an offer. Would he be willing to relocate to Columbus and try to erase the $250,000 debt and make the stores profitable? As an incentive, they offered him a 40 percent share in the stores if he was successful. Thomas enthusiastically accepted the challenge and began creatively marketing the stores, from trading chicken for airtime to devising the iconic wobbling chicken bucket sign (which was eventually used all over the country) to draw customers to the stores.

By 1968 the stores were making record profits and he decided to sell his portion for $1.5 million. He then parlayed that investment and opened his first Wendy's restaurant at the corner of Fifth and Broad Streets in Columbus. He was an overnight sensation. Within ten years he had 1,000 franchises operating around the country. Today the company has 6,500 outlets operating worldwide.

LEGACY

When Wendy's founder Dave Thomas succumbed to a ten-year battle with liver cancer at his Fort Lauderdale home on January 8, 2002, accolades and tributes poured in from industry peers to presidents of the United States.

Steve C. Anderson, the president and chief executive of the National Restaurant Association remembered Thomas for his rags to riches entrepreneurial rise. "More than a popular culture icon, created by his appearance in thousands of television commercials," he wrote, "Dave Thomas lived and worked the American Dream. From humble beginnings he achieved an unprecedented level of success in a highly competitive segment of the restaurant business."[26]

President George W. Bush, who later posthumously awarded the fast food magnate with the Presidential Medal of Freedom, the highest civilian award, recalled his "hard work and great generosity."[27]

But it was Ohio Representative Deborah Pryce, who shares the same home state with the late restaurateur who, in speaking from the floor of the House, may have framed the legacy of Thomas best of all.

"There is no question Dave Thomas will be remembered as a man of humble beginnings who created one of the most successful fast-food chains in the entire world," she began. "He was, indeed, a business giant, a remarkable man. But today I ask that we also remember Dave as a tireless champion for children, for the thousands of children who do not have families to care for them, who do not have permanent homes, and are waiting to be adopted."[28]

A PARADOX

One could be forgiven for trying to make sense of the seeming contradictions of Dave Thomas's life.

How could a boy who was placed for adoption at birth—an adoption that wound up being less than ideal—grow up to be a wildly successful businessman but a mediocre absentee father only to then commit the latter part of his life to advocating for adoption and the value of family life?

Testifying before a congressional committee regarding the importance of creating tax incentives for adoption, Dave offered a partial explanation. "I know firsthand how important it is for every child to have a home and loving family," he declared. "Without a family, I would not be where I am today."[29]

After establishing the Dave Thomas Foundation for Adoption, Thomas travelled the world to raise awareness and encourage families to consider opening their homes and hearts to waiting children. "If I can get just one child a home, it would be better than selling a million hamburgers," he once said. In his typical self-deferential manner he went on to say, "I'm no expert. I'm just a hamburger cook. But I believe in adoption. I believe it is a positive thing. I think everyone deserves a permanent, loving home."[30]

And so, perhaps it's the impact and results of Dave Thomas's advocacy that is his greatest legacy of all. After all, who among us is the perfect parent? Today, countless families who would not otherwise be in a financial position to adopt are able to do so because of legislation like the federal adoption tax credit. Thanks to both Thomas's example and championing, the majority of Fortune 500 corporations now offer adoption benefits like paid time off and reimbursements for travel. He's also helped spark a national conversation about the institution itself, empowering and encouraging other adoptees to be proud of their roots.

"Had I not been adopted," Dave reflected, "I could have ended up as a ward of the state or raised in a county orphanage. So, the way I see it, adoption turned out to be a big plus for me."[31]

THE RISE AND FALL OF ORPHANAGES

For many people, the orphanage, a formal residential institution devoted to the care and nurturing of parentless children, is an image that conjures up a snapshot of a cold and cruel era.

Such a belief is lacking the advantage of historical perspective.

The first formal orphanage dates back to 400 A.D., a byproduct of early Christian believers who adhered to both Old and New Testament directives to care for the fatherless.

"Uphold the rights of the orphan," wrote the prophet Isaiah (1:17). Similarly, James, the brother of Jesus, charged early members of the church to remember that "Religion that God our Father accepts as pure and faultless is this: to look after orphans and widows in their distress and to keep oneself from being polluted by the world" (James 1:27).

Around the same time, the philosopher Plato strongly championed the belief that society was responsible for helping to care for children without parents. "Orphans should be placed under the care of public guardians," he wrote. "Men should have a fear of the loneliness of orphans and of the souls of their departed parents. A man should love the unfortunate orphan of whom he is guardian as if he were his own child. He should be as careful and as diligent in the management of the orphan's property as of his own or even more careful still."[1]

THE CHURCH FILLS THE GAP

It's no surprise then, that it was the Christian Church that took the lead in building and managing the first waves of orphanages. Clergy, often operating out of monasteries, provided the care and nurturing of such children. Over the centuries, institutions for parentless children were often part of hospitals and were privately funded by compassionate-minded individuals and groups. The numbers and need fluctuated based on the cultural happenings of the era, such as wars, epidemics, and natural disasters.

The first recorded orphanage in the United States dates back to before the colonists declared their independence from Great Britain. When the Natchez Indians in Mississippi, upset over French demands for land, slaughtered approximately 230 of the colonists in 1729, dozens of orphaned children were suddenly left needing a place to live. To meet their needs, the Ursuline Sisters, a French Catholic order, transformed their New Orleans school into an orphanage.

A few years later, the German Lutheran missionary August Hermann Francke, who was already overseeing the management of over a hundred orphanages in Europe, helped plant a new one in Ebenezer, Georgia. Francke didn't believe in asking people for money but instead believed the Lord would impress upon Christians the need to support his work, which they did. Inspired by Francke's faith and commitment to the orphans, the Anglican evangelist George Whitefield established a home for parentless children in 1740 in present-day Bethesda, Maryland. He called it "Bethesda," a term that means "house of Mercy."[2]

POST-CIVIL WAR RISE

By the early nineteenth century, dozens of orphanages began springing up around the United States, and by 1860 almost every state had at least one, though many had several. The outbreak of the Civil War saw a sharp increase in demand and the emergence of state-sponsored institutions. Minority groups also began establishing homes for children of their particular race (African-American, Chinese, Japanese, Korean, and Indian Americans).

According to *World Magazine*'s Marvin Olasky, "Orphanage directors during the second half of the nineteenth century saw their mission as not merely furnishing basic material needs but creating model American citizens." He continued, "They tried to instill virtues such as thrift, self-reliance, and sobriety, and to create a capacity for hard work; they believed in busy daily routines and strict discipline."[3]

INDUSTRIAL AGE TRANSFORMATION

As the United States began to transition from primarily an agrarian society to an increasingly industrial one in the first part of the twentieth century, more and more city-based families struggled to provide for their children. Feeling like they had no other choice, these parents, beset by either financial or health concerns, began to drop off their sons and daughters at orphanages. By 1910, American institutions housed well over one hundred thousand children.[4]

In 1909, in response to the rising rate of both child abandonment and the explosion of orphanage construction, President Theodore Roosevelt convened the first White House Conference on the Care of Dependent Children. Before two hundred delegates seated in the East Room, President Roosevelt acknowledged the fact there was no easy solution to the challenges. In doing so, he struck a pragmatic tone.

"The wit of man cannot devise a system so perfect," he said, "that it will work unless it is worked by men both good and wise, and unless outsiders, who take a genuine interest in the matter, also give their aid and exercise their supervision."[5]

The president stressed the value of children being raised in homes rather than institutions. It was decided that part of the solution to the financial hardships single mothers felt and that often led them to relinquish their sons and daughters was to provide them with monetary assistance, thus allowing them to stay home and care for their children. In addition, the foster-care system was developed and launched. Instead of being raised in military/dormitory accommodations, orphans would now be placed, presumably, in the warm and loving environment of a traditional home.

Matthew Crenson, professor emeritus at Johns Hopkins and a scholar who studied the rise and fall of American orphanages for eight years, considers the Roosevelt-led conference to have been a turning point in the cultural debate about the best place for orphaned and neglected children.

"The conference had a phenomenal impact," says Crenson. "It created the momentum that began the drive for the mothers' pension, a precursor to our modern Aid to Families with Dependent Children. It was the watershed event leading to the creation of welfare. The asylum had sought to develop good citizens through the management of an artificially created social environment. The reformers at the White House conference aimed at the management of the real thing. They abandoned the orphanage in order to take up social engineering."[6]

ALTERNATIVE POINT OF VIEW

Over the years, not everyone has been so sure that the move away from traditional orphanages has been a positive development. In the 1990s, then Speaker of the House Newt Gingrich suggested that returning to orphanages could help reduce the welfare rolls. In response, he was pilloried in the press, despite the fact that studies showed children raised in orphanages had a 39 percent higher graduation rate, higher incomes, and lower incarceration rates than others their age.

Furthermore, 85 percent of those who lived in orphanages consider it to have been a favorable experience.

While the traditional orphanage has faded from the American landscape, group homes, such as the well-known Boy's Town in Omaha, Nebraska and many others, still exist. Also known as "Residential Education Facilities," these facilities are heavily regulated.

Given the complexity and differences of opinion surrounding the history of orphanages, the writer John M. Simmons, himself an orphan and now father of eight, including five children adopted from Russia, once offered the following pitch-perfect sentiments. "Orphanages are the only places," he said, "that ever left me feeling empty and full at the same time."[7]

Homes For Children
===WANTED===

A Company of Homeless Children from the East Will Arrive at

McPherson, Friday, September 15.

These children are of various ages and of both sexes, having been thrown friendless upon the world. They come under the auspices of the Children's Aid Society, of New York. They are well-disciplined, having come from various orphanages. The citizens of this community are asked to assist the agent in finding good homes for them. Persons taking these children must be recommended by the local committee. They must treat the children in every way as members of the family, sending them to school, church, Sabbath school and properly clothe them until they are 18 years old. Protestant children placed in Protestant homes and Catholic children in Catholic homes. The following well known citizens have agreed to act as a local committee to aid the agents in securing homes.

Dr. Heaston   H. A. Rowland   C. W. Bachelor
F. A. Vaniman   W. J. Krehbiel   K. Sorenson

Applications must be made to and endorsed by the local committee.

An address will be given by the agents. Come and see the children and hear the address. Distribution will take place at

Opera House, Friday, September 15
at 10:00 a. m. and 2:00 p. m.

Notices like this were handed out to announce the arrival of an Orphan Train.

CHAPTER SEVEN

ART LINKLETTER

When television first took America by storm in the late 1940s and 50s, there were just three national broadcast networks—NBC, CBS, and ABC—and Art Linkletter was a star on two of them (CBS and NBC).

As the host of NBC's *People Are Funny*, Linkletter challenged contestants to carry out creative stunts in exchange for prizes. It was twice nominated for an Emmy. CBS's *House Party*, which enjoyed a twenty-five-year run, was a popular daytime variety/talk show in which he played the part of the curious everyman who seemed to effortlessly find the humorous side of life. He put his subjects at ease and was particularly deft at interviewing children with uproarious results. It was once awarded an Emmy for best daytime talk show.

"The two best interview subjects," he once observed, "are children under ten and people over seventy for the same reason: they say the first thing that comes to their mind. The children don't know what they're saying and the old folks don't care."[1]

When he died on May 26, 2010, just two months shy of his ninety-eighth birthday, Art Linkletter was referred to as someone whose work brought joy and laughter to anyone whose path he crossed. Indeed, his congenial temperament put him in high demand throughout his seventy-plus-year career. But he was not only a gregarious entertainer who hosted popular shows and emceed everything from Kiwanis banquets to the opening of Disneyland. He was also a shrewd businessman with over one hundred business interests from owning and operating a million acre sheep ranch in Australia, to bartering for the film concession in Disneyland to investing in the invention of the hula hoop.

His longtime friend, the comedian Phyllis Diller, said he enjoyed a "full life of fun and goodness," adding he was "an orphan who made it to the top."[2]

Yet, behind the optimism, lightheartedness, and wildly successful entrepreneur lay a more complicated man whose emotions about his birth and adoption ran deep.

A RECURRING FANTASY

Born Arthur Gordon Kelly on July 17, 1912, in Moose Jaw, a small city in south-central Saskatchewan, Linkletter often ruminated about his birthparents and their decision to make an adoption plan for him just days after he was born.

Writing in his autobiography, *Confessions of a Happy Man*, Linkletter pulled back the curtain a bit and reflected on some of his innermost thoughts:

> With the passing of the years, my curiosity about my parents has been dulled to the point where I no longer care. But every man has moments when, no matter how much he is loved or surrounded by love, he is lonely and agonizingly alone. And during those moments, when the world and people and my own loved ones seemed to be as distant as a desert mirage, I thought often about Mr. and Mrs. Kelly of Canada. I

imagined myself driving down an elm-shaded street to a small brown house with a front door and touching the bell with a shaking finger. And they would open the door and their arms would be around me, and they would whisper: "Son, welcome home, son."

But in my heart I knew it would never happen, and it never has. Indeed, as time went on, my curiosity was distorted by rancor, as though there were a chip on my shoulder and I was taunting them to knock it off. "I don't need you any more," I told myself. I've made out all right. You go your way and I'll go mine. I have never been able to silence this inner voice of mine, and I wonder if I ever can.[3]

MR. AND MRS. KELLY

Like many children of his era, Art accidently discovered he was adopted as an infant when he was around eleven years old. He began to notice his parents acted odd whenever an official-looking letter with a Canadian stamp arrived in the mail. If he walked into a room and found them reading one of them, they'd quickly stop what they were doing and put it away.

Curious, he snuck into his parents' room one day and read the letters himself. They were notes from his biological parents inquiring of his well-being. He was hurt and shocked.

"I did not confront the Linkletters with what I considered a deception," he later said. "But as I grew older—and I feel even more strongly about it today—I realized that every adopted child should be told the truth from the earliest possible moment. [Adoptive] parents should never take the chance that a child will learn the truth accidentally, perhaps in some cruel, taunting way from a child."[4]

He would later learn his birthparents traveled from some other city in Canada to Moose Jaw to have him. He never found out if he was born in a hospital or the home of a friend of the Kellys, nor did he ever discover why they chose the remoteness of a city like Moose Jaw. He suspected it had to do with wanting to get away and avoid the embarrassment that accompanied an unwed pregnancy. His birth father was a high school teacher and he speculated the trip was made to protect his employment.

"Perhaps my father would have lost his job if anyone had known why he had to leave home so suddenly and mysteriously," Art said. "Perhaps he was broke at the time. Perhaps neither of them was ready for marriage and parenting. I'm sure it doesn't matter now."[5]

But it did seem to matter to Art Linkletter, even decades later. He learned his biological parents returned to their home city and eventually married and had two other children. This fact left him with more questions. If they planned to marry anyway, why not quickly tie the knot and parent him? Was it something about him they didn't like? His mind raced with possibilities. He felt abandoned, rejected, a castaway.

When nobody tells you anything, irrational thoughts and questions go through an adoptee's mind, young or old.

JOHN AND MARY

The Linkletters of Moose Jaw were one of several couples to register with the local office of Canada's Children's Aid Society and express interest in adopting a child. Believe it or not, Art Linkletter, a man known for his keen curiosity and someone who asked questions all his life, never directly asked his mom or dad why they pursued adoption. But maybe that's because the facts seem rather obvious. John, an insurance salesman at the time, was fifty-one. Mary was forty-two. They lost a baby and were unable to conceive again. Art suspected they were lonely and his arrival filled that void.

By Art's own description, John and Mary Linkletter were not your typical adoptive couple. Fitted with a wooden leg after a childhood accident forced amputation, the tall, heavyset John stood out around town. Although he made his living selling insurance, Art's father was a strong Christian and a fervent evangelist who took every opportunity he could find to tell people about Jesus. When he talked, Art remembers he would "impale the air with his cane as though it were an exclamation point."

Mary, on the other hand, was more quiet and reserved. "A plump, round-faced woman," according to Art, he credited his mother with providing the emotional connection point he so desperately needed in life.[6] One can only imagine, having previously lost a child, the joy she felt to once again have a child to hold and cherish.

"There is one woman whose gentle face is always before me," he once wrote of his mother, "whose voice I hear when there is silence in the house and whose gnarled hands still seem to be shyly touching my shoulders when my thoughts are blue."[7]

A MYSTERIOUS MOVE

For reasons unknown to Art, other than to say that "my mother and father were more rolling stones than rocks," the Linkletters moved from Moose Jaw to Lowell, Massachusetts, shortly after his birth.[8] John gave up the insurance business, and with just a few bags containing all their life's possessions, John, Mary, and little Art boarded a train and headed east. He never again returned to the small Canadian town, though it regularly crossed his mind, especially since he was once named an honorary citizen of the village.

"I have often thought that a return visit to my birthplace might help mend my mental cart," he wrote. "But I am almost afraid to face the inevitable disillusionment of reality. It will not be as I dreamed it to be."[9]

Setting up a home in Lowell, the itinerant Linkletters opened a five and dime store, a curious choice given John's background. "My father had no business sense at all," said Art, "and the store was a dismal failure. At the end of the two years, bankrupt and disillusioned, they packed their bags and migrated thirty-five hundred miles to a rickety little house at Point Fermin, near San Pedro on the southern California coast."[10] There, the roads were unpaved, and all the structures were made of adobe.

SOUTHERN CALIFORNIA BOY

As a young boy growing up in the small town along the Pacific, Art learned at an early age he was expected to help support the family, however small his contribution. "My parents gave me all the love and devotion any boy could expect, but I never had an allowance, and I was expected to pick up whatever I could with odd jobs."[11] One of those "odd jobs" was walking around a local park eating ice cream cones. An ice cream vendor hired him as a plant, believing passersby would be motivated by the power of suggestion. He was right.

Art scrambled and scraped for other jobs like cleaning up yards. In other instances, he created his own opportunities, like the time he visited a lemon-packing plant he discovered piles of discarded lemons. They were rejected because they were sprinkled with specks. Hauling away sacks of them, he and a friend scrubbed the fruit and went door to door selling them for a nickel a dozen. Within a few weeks he hired six other boys to sell for him. Nothing was beneath the young entrepreneur and it felt good to contribute to the welfare of the family.

When he was six or seven, the Linkletters moved again, this time to East San Diego. Unable to afford a home of their own, the family moved into an "old people's home" run by a local church. At the same time, Art's father opened a small shoe repair shop, resurrecting a skill he learned as a young boy. The business was successful enough to allow the family to move into their own house, though it had no indoor bathroom, but an outhouse in the backyard. "The place had three rooms and a path," he joked.[12]

Later in life, Art reflected on how he spent his childhood living in small houses behind large houses, wistfully adding "As I grew older my one fervent wish was to have a street number without a ½ in it."[13]

IN THE SHADOW OF AN EVANGELIST

John Linkletter's passion for the Gospel began to manifest itself more and more as Art grew older. "He had always been intensely religious," his son observed, "but when the message came [a calling from the Lord] he turned preacher in the hellfire and damnation style. He could be violent on the subject of such weaknesses as playing cards, smoking, movies, and liquor."[14]

Art's father also became famous for his long and fervent prayers before meals, causing his son to once remark he was fourteen before a forkful of hot food ever crossed his lips. "My father was no Billy Sunday, but he had a voice like a big league umpire, and when he took on Satan no man could doubt his sincerity."[15]

John Linkletter regularly brought home individuals for dinner whom he was trying to convert, a practice that left Art with humorous memories—and stories. For example, there was the day he learned more about Eddie Smith than Eddie would have cared for him to know.

"Dear Lord, Brother Eddie Smith is our friend for today," his dad began the grace. "Eddie is a pickpocket, and with clever fingers he steals money from honest men's pockets." After they were done praying, an incredulous Eddie asked John who told him he was a pickpocket. "No one told me," his father replied. "You pulled a dollar bill out of my pocket when you got here."

MAKING SENSE OF IT ALL

After discovering he was adopted, Art indicated that while the news startled him to the point of resentment, it also came as something of a relief. As the son of a financially struggling older man and a fiery evangelist at that, the young mind of the boy subconsciously assumed his future would eventually look much the same. But, "Suddenly all this was changed," he said. "Now I could dream...one day, my rich, handsome [biological] father would come in a shiny limousine and take me home to a mansion where there would be no bums nor borrowed bikes nor Salvation Army cast-off clothes."[16]

Linkletter went on to acknowledge the distinction he drew was entirely self-imposed and had they ever found out, it would have been hurtful to his parents. Yet for a youngster in Art's circumstances, he could be excused for thinking such thoughts and later said his father "gave all that he could."

Yet, as he grew older, Art found it a challenge to emotionally connect with John Linkletter. Instead of sitting down with him for warm father-son talks, his dad would often quote Scripture and failed to bring it down from the ethereal or theological to the practical. However, he taught his son an invaluable lesson while the two of them worked in the shoe repair shop. The son noticed the pleasure his father found in the smallest job, noting he only used the best leathers and threads.

"Artie," he once told him, "always do a good job as best you know how. When you grow up, pick a job you like, otherwise you won't do it well. Like me, for instance, I like to mend shoes."

OFF ON AN ADVENTURE

In high school, Art held a variety of positions with the San Diego YMCA, from picking up wet towels to serving as a summer camp counselor, where he famously coached a very young Ted Williams in baseball. It was at the Y he met Dave Bomberger, an executive with the organization. Dave became a second father to Art, encouraging him both professionally and personally. Thanks to Dave, Art gained confidence and developed practical skills for life. For example, his first introduction to broadcasting took place at the YMCA's Camp Marston on July 26, 1928. It was there, in an effort to entertain campers, that, unbeknownst to the kids around the campfire, he impersonated the radio commentator for a broadcast of a prize fight they were listening to between then heavyweight champ Gene Tunney and Tom Heeney. Broadcasting in a shack out of sight, Linkletter's color commentary convinced everyone within earshot they were listening to the real thing. Unfortunately, in his version, he had Heeney beating Tunney when it was actually the other way around. When the truth was learned the next day, all the bets had to be reversed. Still, it was there under the wing of the YMCA and Bomberger that he discovered his love for the magic and power of the microphone.

By the time high school graduation rolled around in June of 1929, Art was ready for an adventure. He was seventeen and decided, along with a friend, Denver Fox, to take off on a journey to see America.

"Among other things," Art wrote, "we learned to chisel rides on freight trains, outwit the railroad bulls, cook stews with the bindle stiffs, and never argue with a gun."[17]

Over the course of the next six months, the two boys found enough work along the way to eat, sleep, and see the sights. "Along the route," Art remembered, "I met hundreds of people—scoundrels and heroes, laborers and bosses, geniuses and nitwits—and there was not one who did not have something to give. I learned no man has to starve if he's willing to work and you make your own horizons. Best of all, my mind was storing up countless little facts about people which would later be useful on my radio and television shows."[18]

RADIO COMES CALLING

Back in California, Linkletter enrolled at San Diego State University, majoring in English. A series of random jobs followed including one as a fake gambler in a Mexican casino watching for cheaters. As a junior, he landed a job as a part-time announcer at radio station KGB where he helped launch one of the "every-man on the street" interview programs. He was eventually promoted to chief announcer and program director. Art finally found his path to his life's work in broadcasting.

After an on-again, off-again courtship, Art married Lois Foerster on November 28, 1935, at Grace Lutheran Church. They had five children; Arthur Jack, who died in 2007 of lymphoma, Dawn, Robert, who died in a car accident in 1980, Sharon, and Diane, who committed a drug-influenced suicide in 1969. Despite all the tragedy surrounding their children, the Linkletters enjoyed a happy, nearly seventy-five-year marriage.

THE FIVE LINKS

According to Sharon, life in the large, white Georgian house at 219 South Mapleton Drive in the celebrity-laden Los Angeles neighborhood of Holmby Hills was comfortable but very normal. "We felt we were very normal kids. They didn't indulge us. My father always taught us the value of a dollar," she said. "He would count out the dollar bills for emphasis."[19]

It was son Jack's impromptu interview with his father in his study after the first day of kindergarten that inspired the child interview section of *House Party*.

"Jack, what did you do today?" asked Art.

"I went to school for the first time," said Jack.

"How did you like it?"

"I'm not going back."

"Why aren't you going back?"

"Because I can't read, I can't write, and they won't let me talk."[20]

The Linkletter kids, whom Art referred to as "The Links," trained to identify opportunities, were known to sometimes make things happen on their own, however ethically questionable the circumstances. Aware that tourists were regularly stopping to take pictures of their house, the Linkletter kids picked the neighbor's flowers and sold them out of their wagon.

"They put an end to that as soon as my parents found out," said Sharon with a laugh.[21]

Growing up, Sharon, whose best friend was another neighbor girl, Liza Minelli, remembers a father who deeply loved his family, although he sometimes found it difficult to emotionally connect. "When my sister Diane died, my father didn't talk much about it. Instead, he turned it into a crusade, traveling the country and talking about the evils of drug abuse."[22]

However, Sharon does remember the Linkletters financially supporting foster children all over the world, an obvious though silent nod to his past. "My dad didn't talk much, if at all, about his own adoption," she said. "But whenever we traveled, he would make a point for us to visit with these children the family was supporting. It made a big impression on me."[23]

ADOPTION'S INFLUENCE

The fullness of Art Linkletter's life would fill pages and pages, but this story is not so much about the totality of Art's success, but rather the impact and role his adoption in Moose Jaw played in it. Clearly, it was a factor, and a major one at that. Although emotionally distant at times, Art enjoyed the tender care of parents who, while struggling to communicate their love for him, laid a foundation for him in ways big and small. From all those dinners with strangers to living in the midst of aging people, Art learned how to talk with anyone about anything, anywhere. From sitting by his father in his shoe shop, he learned the importance of pursuing your passion, not a salary.

For reasons that Art never acknowledged, John Linkletter was unable to attend his and Lois's wedding, though his mother, Mary did participate. The cobbler, though, sent a telegram to Lois, which read in part:

> We are looking forward to a visit from you and Mr. Link. Or in other words our darling boy, Artie. He will always be "dear Artie" to me. Well, dear Lois, we are continuously praying the dear Lord to Bless you both. To honor and obey Him insures success and carries a promise of long life. Psalm 91:16 ["With long life I will satisfy him…"]. Read that Psalm, won't you dear?
>
> Bushels of love,
> Old Papa[24]

John and Mary Linkletter's prayer for a baby was answered with Art's arrival in 1912 and "Old Papa's" prayer in 1935 was likewise answered given Art and Lois's near seventy-five-year union.

CHAPTER EIGHT

GERALD FORD

The scene seems straight out of a movie.

It's just past noon on a weekday afternoon in the spring of 1930. The location is Bill's Place, a popular diner located on Hall Street, directly across from South High School in Grand Rapids, Michigan. Most of the lunch crowd has been served and are now settled in their seats. A cacophony of steady conversation fills the air in the room.

Several young, apron-clad servers are hustling back and forth between the tables and the kitchen, carrying plates of food, filling and refilling water glasses and coffee cups. The restaurant's owner, Bill Skougis, an enthusiastic booster for the high school who likes to hire athletes to serve in his establishment, is overseeing it all. He pays $2 a week for part-time work and provides free meals, a fair deal for hungry students of parents struggling their way through the Great Depression.

Behind the counter is one of his most recent hires. His name is Gerald Ford, the future thirty-eighth president of the United States. He's seventeen years old and a junior. Jerry, as he's known to his friends, is handsome and well-liked, the captain of the football team. Since everyone has been served and nobody is arriving anymore, there's a lull in the action and Ford looks up to notice a tall, well-dressed man standing alone by the door. He's apparently not looking to be seated. He's just standing—and staring.

Ford carries on with his duties and looks up again to find the gentleman studying him. It makes him uneasy. Finally, the man walks from the door to the counter and directly up to the seventeen-year-old Ford.

"Are you Leslie King?" the man asks Jerry.

"No," Ford replied.

"Are you Jerry Ford?" he then asks.

"Yes," answers the young man, a perplexed look washing across his face.

"You're Leslie King. I'm your father. You don't know me. I'm in town with my wife, and I would like to take you out for lunch."[1]

INITIAL INFATUATION

Leslie King first met Gerald Ford's mother, Dorothy Gardner, while visiting his sister Marietta at Knox College, a small liberal arts school in Knoxville, Illinois. It was the spring of 1912. Leslie was thirty years of age and Dorothy was ten years his junior. According to those who knew them, it was love at first sight. King impressed the attractive brunette collegian with his dreams and plans for the future. He was a man ready to rise and eager to build a life with his new love.

In 1900, the King family's wealth was estimated to be approximately ten million dollars, or nearly two hundred and fifty million in today's dollars. Leslie's father was Charles Henry King, an Omaha businessman who amassed his fortune in conjunction with the expansion of the transcontinental railroad. Various business interests, including the Omaha Wool and Storage Company, led Mr. King to also help establish several cities in Nebraska and Wyoming.

Convinced he and Dorothy were meant for one another, Leslie wrote her father, Levi Gardner, asking his permission to marry her. Though not nearly as wealthy as the Kings, the Gardners were a prominent family of Harvard, Illinois. Mr. Gardner had been the town's mayor and owned a successful furniture store and real estate business. His wife, Adele, hailed from the family that founded the town. Loving and protective parents, the Gardners wanted to know more about Leslie. Did he have the means to care for her? He assured them he had considerable savings (thirty-five thousand dollars) and earned $150 a month working at the family's wool business. The parents enthusiastically gave their blessing. After they were married, he moved the two of them into their own cozy cottage. Their future was bright.

The wedding, just months later on September 17, 1912, was all the talk of Harvard. "Many Harvard people met the young Omaha man who has won one of the most popular of Harvard young ladies as his bride," reported the *Harvard Herald*. "He is a young man of good repute and is a highly regarded business man."[2]

Sadly, neither claim would wind up being true.

RAGE AND ABUSE

It was only ten days after the wedding, while on their honeymoon at the Multnomah Hotel in Portland, Oregon, when Leslie first struck Dorothy. He was convinced she had flirted with a man on the elevator. She insisted she simply nodded to acknowledge his greeting. In response, according to court documents eventually filed, Leslie "became enraged…and set upon her, called her vile and insulting names…struck and slapped her in the face and about the head."[3]

Leslie allegedly struck and kicked her again the very next day as they took the train from San Francisco to Los Angeles. His red-hot temper raged again just days later. Each time he apologized and she accepted.

Upon arriving back in Omaha, Dorothy learned there would be no cottage, but instead they would be living with his parents in the large family home on Woolworth Ave. More fights and abuse ensued. Leslie ordered his wife to leave, which she did, returning home to her parents in Harvard. Days later, Leslie arrived, pleading for Dorothy's forgiveness.

Once again, she forgave him.

Returning to Omaha, the couple moved into a basement apartment. Leslie confided he was deeply in debt. The dark, cramped living quarters was all he could afford. Although he promised to take her home for Christmas, such a trip was now out of the question due to their crippled finances. When Dorothy's father sent money for the tickets, Leslie refused to go. More episodes of abuse followed.

In the midst of all the depression and dysfunction, Dorothy discovered she was pregnant. Her mother asked to come for the birth, which she did, and on July 14, 1913, the hottest day of the year in Omaha, her baby boy was born.

Leslie insisted he be named after him.

THE ESCAPE

One would expect the arrival of a new baby into a home to bring love and joy into it, but then again, babies, like money and fame, often magnify preexisting problems. Such was the case in the birth of Gerald Ford. Just one day after the baby's arrival, Leslie was ranting and raving again at his wife. The doctor ordered him to back off and give his wife time to rest and recover. He also requested that a nurse remain in the house around the clock. In turn, the new father demanded both the nurse and the mother-in-law leave, even threatening to shoot his wife if they didn't.

Both refused and held their ground.

An emergency telegram was sent to Mr. Gardner, who took the next train and arrived hoping to mediate the crisis. Leslie admitted to him separation was a good idea. But immediately after Levi Gardner departed, Leslie's mood changed again. At one point, he threatened everyone there—mother, baby, and mother-in-law—with a butcher's knife. The police were called. Tensions cooled, but then soon flared up once more. Again, Mr. Gardner was summoned. He returned, but this time was unable to see his daughter because Leslie had just gotten a court order blocking them from seeing her.

The situation was growing desperate.

Unbeknownst to Leslie, Dorothy phoned a lawyer. What should she do? The attorney gave her some advice that very well may have saved the future president's life.

Dorothy was told to leave with the baby—immediately.

And so with the nurse watching out for her mentally unstable husband, Dorothy wrapped her little boy in a blanket and slipped quickly and quietly out of the house. She didn't even stop to pack a bag. Running quickly down Woolworth Avenue in the heat of summer, she hailed a carriage which took her out of the city and across the Nebraska/Iowa border to the city of Council Bluffs. There she met up with her parents and together the four of them boarded a train and headed for Chicago.

A FRESH START

Dorothy filed for divorce, and by December of 1913 an Omaha court found Leslie King "guilty of extreme cruelty" and ordered him to pay three thousand dollars for back alimony and twenty-five dollars a month for child support. Furthermore, Dorothy, who was now living with her sister and brother-in-law in Oak Park, Illinois, was awarded full custody of her little boy. King refused to pay a dime. When a court tried to seize his assets, it was discovered he was broke. His father, Charles King, agreed to pay the monthly child support for his paternal grandson, a practice he would continue until the stock market crash of 1929 wiped out the family's fortune.

Because Dorothy Gardner's parents felt as though their daughter's divorce would somehow bring shame to the family back in Harvard, they decided to relocate to Grand Rapids, Michigan, and invite their daughter and grandson to move in with them. At the early part of the twentieth century, the River City was a diverse metropolis of opportunity. Entrepreneurs abounded along with hundreds of manufacturing plants. But according to Ford's biographer, James Cannon, in Grand Rapids in the teens and twenties, "A boy could grow up there with his days filled with sunshine—playing baseball, fishing in the river, swimming at the beach, and ice skating in the winter."[4]

The unconventional family of four quickly settled into their new lives at 457 Lafayette Street, still harboring resentment from their wounds in Omaha, but relieved to finally find domestic peace.

A FATEFUL MEETING AT CHURCH

In 1915, Gerald Ford Sr. was twenty-four years old and making a good living selling paint and varnish to the many furniture manufacturing plants in Grand Rapids. Never married, he decided to attend a social event for singles at the Grace Episcopal Church. It was there he met Dorothy. A near year-long courtship followed, and they were married on February 1, 1916.

In so many ways, Gerald Ford was everything Leslie King was not. He was disciplined, courteous, respectful, steady, and even-tempered. He was conservative, too, a faithful church attender. He meant what he said and said what he meant. He loved children and immediately accepted his new stepson as his own, quickly bonding.

FATHER AND SON

"He was the father I grew up to believe was my father, the father I loved and learned from and respected. He was my dad," said the former president of Gerald Ford Sr.[5] Ford's parents waited until he was thirteen to explain to him about the divorce and remarriage.

"It didn't make a big impression on me at the time," he would later say. "I guess I didn't understand exactly what a stepfather was. Dad and I had the closest, most intimate relationship. We acted alike. We had the same interests. I thought we looked alike."[6]

Unlike many adopted children, Ford didn't have much interest in meeting his biological father. "I had never met the man she said was my father," he reflected. "I didn't know where he lived, couldn't have cared less about him. Because I was as happy a young man as you could find."[7]

He grew further reflective: "I was very lucky. I was so lucky that my mother divorced my [biological] father, who I hate to say was a bad person in many respects. She had a lot of guts to get out of that situation. When she moved to Grand Rapids and married my stepfather, that was just pure luck. We had a tremendous relationship, Dad and I. My stepfather had so much love for me, if not more, than his own three sons."[8]

GROWING UP IN GRAND RAPIDS

Gerald eventually gained three brothers, Tom (1918), Dick (1924) and Jim (1927). Ford's father was intentional with him and went to great effort to spend concentrated time with each of his sons. "Dad," Ford recalled with fondness, "with some other men, owned a cabin on the Little South Branch of the Peter Marquette River, and he would take me there to fish, and we would walk in the woods and in the sunlight."[9]

Together, with their dad, the Ford boys found their second homes on the diamond, gridiron, and basketball court. Their father saw sports as more than mere recreation. "He believed sports taught you how to live," President Ford wrote, "how to compete but always by the rules, how to be part of a team, how to win, how to lose and come back and try again."[10]

The mood inside the Ford home was fun, but morally centered. "He [my father] drilled into me the importance of honesty," said Ford. "Whatever happened, you were honest. Dad and Mother had three rules: Tell the truth, work hard and come to dinner on time. Woe to any of us who violated those rules."[11]

The boys' father modeled those standards outside the home while running his business, the Ford Paint and Varnish Company. When the economy took a nosedive and companies were closing all over the city, Gerald Sr. announced to his employees he was going to keep them employed, but cut their pay—and his. "We can pay you five dollars a week to keep you in groceries, and that's what I will pay myself," he told them. "When times get better, we will make up the difference between the $5 and your regular pay, however long it takes."[12]

A MOTHER'S WISDOM

Early on in his life, Dorothy recognized Gerald inherited his biological father's fiery temper, and she was determined to try and cure him of the bad habit. Given the tragic consequences of Leslie's rage, she decided to be creative and accentuate the positive side of an even-keeled person. Just as soon as he was old enough to read, she made him memorize Rudyard Kipling's famous poem, "If," which read, in part:

1. If you can keep your head when all about you
2. Are losing theirs and blaming it on you,
3. If you can trust yourself when all men doubt you,
4. But make allowance for their doubting too;
5. If you can wait and not be tired by waiting,
6. Or being lied about, don't deal in lies,
7. Or being hated, don't give way to hating,
8. And yet don't look too good, nor talk too wise:
9. If you can dream—and not make dreams your master;
10. If you can think—and not make thoughts your aim;
11. If you can meet with Triumph and Disaster
12. And treat those two impostors just the same;
13. If you can bear to hear the truth you've spoken
14. Twisted by knaves to make a trap for fools,
15. Or watch the things you gave your life to, broken,
16. And stoop and build 'em up with worn-out tools:
17. … Yours is the Earth and everything that's in it,
18. And—which is more—you'll be a Man, my son.[13]

POSITIVE INFLUENCES

For a young Gerald Ford, his twelfth birthday opened a world he was eagerly awaiting: membership in the Boy Scouts. Old enough to finally enroll, the outdoor enthusiast quickly embraced all things scouting with Troop 15 in Grand Rapids. His scoutmaster was Chuck Kindel, a man he greatly admired and who saw in him the seeds of a successful life. "I could tell right off," Chuck said years later, "that Jerry would become an important person."[14] He earned his Eagle badge, scouting's highest honor, in 1927, earning twenty-seven merit badges. It was one of his first great accomplishments and one that would stick with him the rest of his life.

"One of the proudest moments of my life came in the court of honor when I was awarded the Eagle Scout badge," he told a group of Boy Scouts, shortly after being sworn in as president. "I still have that badge. It is a treasured possession. It is a reminder of some of the basic, good things about our country and a reminder of some of the simple but vital values that can make life productive and very rewarding."[15]

Clifford Gettings, Ford's football coach at South High School, was another significant source of influence on the young man's life.

"Coach Gettings was a stern taskmaster," Ford recalled. "I spent hours learning from him how to snap the ball back, leading a tailback a step in the direction he was going to run, putting it high and soft for a fullback coming."[16] What Ford remembered most of all about Coach Gettings, however, was the transcendent lesson he taught him about behavior on or off the field.

"You play to win," he would say. "You give it everything you've got, but you always play within the rules."[17]

CONFRONTING THE PAST, LOOKING AHEAD

When Leslie King appeared sixteen years after last seeing his son inside Bill's Place, Gerald Ford was understandably rattled, but agreed to meet with him. The lunch was anticlimactic. His biological father didn't have any good answers for his son's questions. How could he have acted like he did? Why didn't he ever pay his mother the support the court ordered? In the end, King asked if Gerald was interested in coming to live with them. He flat out declined. Why would he want to do that? He was enjoying his life in Grand Rapids with the only parents he ever knew. They quickly parted ways and would only see one another sporadically until King's death in 1941 at the age of fifty-six.

Arriving home that night, Jerry was anxious about how to tell his parents what happened. "Telling them (my mom and dad) was one of the most difficult experiences of my life. They did understand. They consoled me and showed in every way that they loved me."[18]

Later that night, though, he tossed and turned. Rage and resentment ran through his veins. "Nothing could erase the image I gained of my [biological] father that day—a carefree, well-to-do man who really didn't gave a d--- about the hopes and dreams of his son."[19]

Staring into the silent darkness, Ford remembered one of the many techniques his mother taught him when trying to confront and curtail his temper. Through his tears he began reciting over and over from memory Proverbs 3:5–6:

> Trust in the Lord with all your heart, and do not lean on your
> own understanding. In all your ways acknowledge him, and
> he will make straight your paths.

A FAST RISE

Thanks in large part to the generosity of a high school administrator who believed in him, Gerald Ford Jr. was able to attend the University of Michigan, where he was voted the most valuable player of their football team in his senior year. In 1935, he went on to coach boxing and football at Yale and eventually made his way into their law school, from which he graduated in 1941. With the outbreak of World War II in December, he received a commission in the United States Navy and spent the vast majority of his service on the USS *Monterey* aircraft carrier.

After the war, Gerald Ford was introduced to Elizabeth Bloomer Warren, a one-time fashion model and dance instructor. They began dating and eventually married two weeks before her new husband was elected to the House of Representatives for their home district in Grand Rapids. For part of their honeymoon the couple campaigned at a political rally at a University of Michigan football game.

Ford served with distinction in the House of Representatives for the next twenty-five years before being tapped to serve as Richard Nixon's vice president after Spiro Agnew was forced to resign for tax evasion in 1973 and, ultimately, assuming the presidency in August of 1974 following Richard Nixon's resignation.

HEALER

After being sworn in by Supreme Court Chief Justice Warren Burger as the nation's thirty-eighth president, Gerald Ford stood before several hundred people inside the East Room of the White House and tens of millions more on national television. He knew job number one was to try and restore trust and decency to a republic deeply battered by the controversy surrounding the Watergate scandal.

"My fellow Americans," he declared, "our long national nightmare is over ... Our Constitution works; our great Republic is a government of laws and not of men. Here the people rule. But there is a higher Power, by whatever name we honor Him, who ordains not only righteousness but love, not only justice but mercy."[20] A month later he pardoned Nixon. He did so not because he thought Nixon was innocent, but instead to spare the country the pain and drama of a long drawn out trial. It was a selfless act, really, because it was an unpopular decision that all but ensured he wouldn't be elected in 1976.

At his core, until his death on December 26, 2006, at the age of ninety-three, Gerald Ford was an optimist who looked for the best in everyone and everything, a trait his father modeled for him as a young boy. "Everybody has more good things about them than bad things," he would say. "If you accentuate the good things in dealing with a person, you can like him even though he or she has some bad qualities. If you have that attitude, you never hate anybody."[21]

When he died, *Wall Street Journal* columnist and former speechwriter Peggy Noonan acknowledged those very same traits. "He didn't indulge his angers and appetites," she wrote the day of his death. "He seems to have thought, in the end, that such indulgence was for sissies—it wasn't manly. He was sober-minded, solid, respecting, and deserving of respect. And at that terrible time, after Watergate, he picked up the pieces and then threw himself on the grenade."[22]

How fitting that a boy whose first weeks of life were framed by struggle, strife, and hurt would one day rise to a position where he would be called on to help lead his nation in a time of constitutional crisis. It was almost as if he had been groomed for the moment from the very beginning, which of course, he had.

"We were lucky to have him," concluded Peggy Noonan. "We were really lucky to have him."[23]

CHAPTER NINE

GEORGE WASHINGTON CARVER

W hen it comes to piecing together the early life of George Washington Carver, one of America's most well-known agricultural researchers and scientists, there are almost as many questions as there are answers.

What we do know is George was born to a woman named Mary, a slave owned by Moses and Susan Carver of Diamond Grove, Missouri. Mary joined the Carvers as a thirteen-year-old girl in 1855. The family were homesteaders who claimed their farm in the late 1830s. It eventually grew to 240 acres. Their primary crop was Indian corn, but they also grew oats, wheat, and Irish potatoes, and raised livestock. It was considered a successful and prosperous property, so much so they decided in 1855 they needed more help to maintain the family business.

Although morally opposed to slavery (a family claim that some historians dispute), the Carvers nevertheless decided to purchase Mary. Roy Porter, a grandnephew of the Carvers, contended that Moses struggled mightily with his decision to join the ranks of slave ownership, remarking that "[Moses] hoped that his ownership of a slave would not be written in heaven against him at the time of his death."[1]

Upon Mary's arrival, she cooked, cleaned house, and tackled numerous other chores.

In time, she also conceived and gave birth to five children.

And here is where the details grow murky.

As for when he was actually born, George Washington Carver would contend for the majority of his life he arrived in either 1864 or 1865.

"I was born about the close of the great Civil War," he once said with great certainty and specificity. "It was in a little one-roomed log shanty, on the home of Mr. Moses Carver, a German by birth and the owner of my mother, my father being the property of Mr. Grant, who owned the adjoining plantation."[2]

Yet, when asked by the popular journalist Ernie Pyle shortly before his death in 1943, Carver suggested he was no longer so sure. "I don't know," he said flatly. "I was born into slavery. I was chattel. We were all chattels...I don't know how old I am."[3]

After historians at the National Park Service completed a six-year investigation in 1957 involving U.S. Census records, Carver's birth was pronounced to be July 12, 1860. Subsequent biographers have continued to debate the question, each coming to different conclusions.

As for the identity of his biological father?

Again, the details are either foggy or downright speculative.

Carver's contention that his birthfather was an enslaved African-American owned by James Grant has never been confirmed, though it does seem likely. As a young boy, he was told his biological dad died in an accident. "My father was killed while hauling wood with an ox team," he said. "In some way he fell from the load, under the wagon, both wheels passing over him."[4]

Some historians have suggested George's father wasn't another slave but actually Moses Carver, Mary's owner. But there's no evidence to corroborate such a claim. George's older brother, Jim, had lighter skin, leading some to speculate his birthfather was white. Of the three older sisters, only one survived long enough to live with George.

But let's dig a little deeper.

Were George's biological parents married? Again, it's impossible to know for sure, but it's unlikely. If they were, they would have had to have entered into what was then known as an "abroad marriage"—a union codified, even informally, outside the boundaries of the plantation. But Missouri law only began to recognize slave marriages in 1865 after the state's constitution outlawed slavery itself, so most historians don't believe they were married.

KIDNAPPED, RANSOMED, & RESCUED

The mysterious origins of George Washington Carver's life are further complicated by what happened just six weeks after his birth, whether in 1860, 1864, or 1865. According to the story he was told, a group of Confederate guerilla warfare soldiers, known as bushwhackers, kidnapped George along with his mother and sister, taking them to Arkansas. There they planned to sell them. His older brother somehow managed to escape prior to the kidnapping.

"Bushwhacking" was particularly popular in rural Missouri during the Civil War. Historians have described it as a "war within a war" and that also reflected the sharp differences between Union and Confederate forces.

In response to the kidnapping, the Carvers hired some soldiers to go track down and rescue the family. The infant George was found and returned after Moses agreed to the demands of the bushwhackers—a $300 racehorse.[5] But Mary was never located.

Once again, history is rife with speculation regarding the incident.

Did it really happen in the dramatic way George was told? It wasn't completely far-fetched. At the height of the slavery debate, vigilante groups were known to pull off such attacks and demand excessive ransoms. But, might Mary, weary of years of servitude, exacerbated by the unrelenting sorrow of losing two of her daughters, have simply escaped on her own? Is it plausible she would have voluntarily given up relationship and contact with her sons and daughter in exchange for her freedom and theirs? Perhaps not, but why wasn't her body ever found? Even George acknowledged the confusion and uncertainty surrounding the incident. He was once told his mother and sister were spotted being led away. "There are now so many conflicting reports concerning them," he later wrote, "I dare not say if they are dead or alive."[6]

In the end, it's impossible to know what exactly happened. Such is just one of the countless consequences stemming from the tragic era of slavery. Black women were especially vulnerable and dispensable.

Yet, we *do know* both Jim and George, now suddenly orphaned, were returned to the Carver homestead. Without their mother and with slaves being freed in Missouri in 1865, the Carvers changed their names. "Carver's George" became "George Carver" and "Carver's Jim" became "Jim Carver."

From the best we can tell, neither of the two boys would ever meet their biological father nor see their mother again. Since George and his mom were together for less than two months, George always yearned to know more about her. "What little I learned *about* my mother," he once wrote, "was that she was a very remarkable woman from many angles."[7]

Life for the Carver boys was changing, and dramatically so. Moses and Susan Carver, now fifty-two and fifty years of age, respectively, moved the two boys from the bareness of their slave quarters into the comfort of their own home. There they subsequently raised them as they would sons of their own. According to George, "My brother James and I grew up together, sharing each other's sorrows on the splendid farm owned by Mr. Carver."[8]

A CHALLENGING CHILDHOOD

Susan's first challenge, though, was to nurse George back to health. He returned from captivity gravely ill with a bad case of whooping cough. At the time, the illness (pertussis) was fatally striking many youngsters in the area. Susan successfully treated the cough with juice she squeezed from a roasted red onion and sweetened with sugar.

Unfortunately, George's first illness foreshadowed a series of health challenges that would follow him throughout his lifetime. Looking back at his childhood bouts with sickness, Dr. Carver remarked, "My body was very feeble and it was a constant warfare between life and death to see who would gain the mastery." He would also struggle with a weak voice. "I have to be exceedingly careful with my throat," he said. "I have a very, very weak throat, and it gives away on me if I'm not careful."[9]

PLANTING SEEDS, LITERALLY AND FIGURATIVELY

George's frailty and chronic poor health prompted his step-parents to modify what was expected of him around the farm. He tired easily, even after just minor exertion. "To carry a little water from the spring in a gallon pail and bring in a few chips and keep the fire going was about all I would do," Carver recalled.[10] While his brother Jim tackled the more strenuous activities, George assisted his mother. He learned to cook, wash, iron, knit, crochet, sew, and tend to the flower beds.

The reduced schedule and lighter duties also afforded him time to wander the woods and study the wonders of nature, a hobby and habit he enthusiastically embraced. It was there he began to develop his curiosity for botany. He would walk and sit for hours, stopping to study trees, rocks, and insects. The exposure to the majesty of creation also began to foster his personal faith.

"As a very small boy exploring the almost virgin woods of the old Carver place," he said, "I had the impression someone had just been there ahead of me. Things were so orderly, so clean, so harmoniously beautiful. A few years later in these same woods I was to understand the meaning of this boyish impression. Because I was practically overwhelmed with the sense of some Great Presence. Not only had someone been there. Someone was there."[11]

CONVERSION TO CHRISTIANITY

For George Washington Carver, that someone, of course, was Jesus Christ. In 1931, Carver wrote of his conversion to Christianity to a friend:

> I was just a mere boy when converted, hardly ten years old. There isn't much of a story to it. God just came into my heart one

afternoon while I was alone in the "loft" of our big barn while I was shelling corn to carry to the mill to be ground into meal.

A dear little white boy, one of our neighbors, about my age came by one Saturday morning, and in talking and playing he told me he was going to Sunday school tomorrow morning. I was eager to know what a Sunday school was. He said they sang hymns and prayed. I asked him what prayer was and what they said. I do not remember what he said; only remember that as soon as he left I climbed up into the "loft," knelt down by the barrel of corn and prayed as best I could. I do not remember what I said. I only recall that I felt so good that I prayed several times before I quit.

My brother and myself were the only colored children in that neighborhood and of course, we could not go to church or Sunday school, or school of any kind.

That was my simple conversion, and I have tried to keep the faith.[12]

To Carver, all of creation pointed to the reality of a Creator. It was that simple and that profound. "Years later when I read in the Scripture, 'In Him we live and move and have our being (Acts 17:28),' I knew what the writer meant. Never since have I been without the consciousness of the Creator speaking to me..."[13]

His step-parents seemed to encourage his passion, allowing him the time to explore and pursue his love of nature. There's evidence to suggest George's stepfather, Moses, also appreciated the outdoors and everything in it, often walking around with a rooster perched on his shoulders. "[My stepfather] had an uncanny rapport with animals," observed George.[14]

The boy who would grow up to be nicknamed the "cook stove chemist," had an insatiable appetite for science. "I literally lived in the woods," he said. "I wanted to know every strange stone, flower, insect, bird, or beast."[15] In September of 1940, just three years before his death, he further connected his passion with his personal faith, writing, "I remember as a boy a little expression that has lingered with me all through life. It said that 'Flowers were the sweetest thing that God ever made and forgot to put a soul into it.' It was one of the things that impressed me so very much that I always remembered it, but as I grow older and study plant life, I am convinced that God didn't forget to do anything that was worthwhile."[16]

A THIRST FOR KNOWLEDGE

The absence of any black schools in the area prevented George and his brother from initially receiving a traditional classroom education. Susan did her best to educate the boys at home, but it soon became obvious she was ill-equipped to give them what they needed. "I had an inordinate desire for knowledge, and especially music, painting, flowers, and the sciences, algebra being one of my favorite studies," George remembered. The Carvers, he acknowledged, "were very kind to me and I thank them so much for my home training. They encouraged me to secure knowledge, helping me all they could, but this was quite limited."[17]

Just one mile from the Carver farm was the Locus Grove School. Moses and Susan attempted to enroll the eleven-year-old but were eventually rejected because of their color. The Carvers arranged for one of the white teachers from Locus Grove to come tutor the boys.

A year later, the family arranged for George to attend what was called the "Neosho Colored School" in Neosho, Missouri, a town eight miles from the family farm. It was a large town with over two thousand people and contained lots of industry. The school housed between twenty-five to forty children who ranged in age between five and twenty-one. It wasn't easy for the Carvers to say good-bye to the boys. Moses missed playing his fiddle for them, but the couple felt strongly about the need for them to receive an education and knew they were unable to give it to them. The boys returned for visits to the Carver farm, but they never again lived there full-time.

CULTURAL ADJUSTMENT

In Neosho, the youngster lived with Andrew and Mariah Watkins, a black couple who had a house next door to the school. He did domestic chores to pay for his room and board. It was in Neosho that George began to see what was really possible. Living with "Aunt Mariah" and "Uncle Andy," George bonded over the exploration and study of medicinal herbs. The Watkins also gave him his first Bible (which he used and cherished the rest of his life), and they took him to church.

Others served to influence George in Neosho. Also living with the Watkins was a formerly enslaved girl named Libby. She successfully transitioned to life as a free person, and so the family would tell George to "learn all you can, then be like Libby. Go out in the world and give your learning back to our people."[18] From Libby he would draw the inspiration that would later lead to him helping many black farmers to use their farms more wisely.

For the first time in his life, George was a black boy living in a black home. He was no longer a minority. It was an empowering feeling, and the exposure and experience filled him with self-confidence.

After nearly two years in Neosho, George sought additional schooling in various towns in Kansas, including Fort Scott, Olathe, Paola, and finally, Minneapolis, Kansas. In Olathe he lived with Ben and Lucy Seymour, another black couple who became surrogate parents in the same way the Watkins did in Neosho.

His previous domestic work experience paid off as he supported himself with a series of odd jobs, cooking, and cleaning. After the Seymours left for Minneapolis, George decided to tag along. It was in Minneapolis where he established his own laundry business and graduated from high school. While there he also joined a Presbyterian church and began to deepen his faith. Tragedy struck George in 1883 when his brother Jim died of smallpox in Seneca, Missouri.

APPLICATION AND REJECTION

George was ecstatic when his application for admission to nearby Highlands University, a school run by the Presbyterian Church, was accepted. His dreams were soon thwarted, however, when he showed up and administration officials realized he was black. Fearful that donors would object to having an African-American student on campus, he was denied entrance.

Dejected, George decided to try his hand at homesteading and settled on 160 acres in Beeler, Kansas. Perhaps he'd never get his chance to pursue higher education and his future was to be the familiar setting of a farm. But, unlike the Carver farm, his land outside Beeler was less than ideal. It had no trees for building and no river or creek for water. Digging a well proved fruitless. He later discovered the area was prone to extreme weather—droughts in the summer and blizzards in the winter. Furthermore, he was one of the few minorities in the area and found the area difficult to navigate.

Within three years, George had abandoned his land and relocated to Winterset, Iowa, and took a job as a cook at the Nicholas Hotel. He also began to attend church where he met John and Helen Milholland, an older white couple with whom he began to forge a warm and meaningful relationship. The Milhollands saw great potential in George and strongly recommended he consider going back to school. Shortly thereafter, he gained admittance to Simpson College in Indianola, Iowa. He studied art and piano, but only for a year. He transferred to Iowa State Agricultural College in Ames, Iowa, after an art teacher at Simpson, recognizing his love of flowers, encouraged him to study botany.

Over the course of his life, George came to see and appreciate the significance of reaching out to others for counsel and advice. From the Carvers to the Seymours, the Watkins and now the Milhollands, the developing botanist was shaped and nurtured by a series of mentoring couples who only had his best interest at heart.

THE PLANT DOCTOR COMES OF AGE

At Iowa State, George found his true calling and upon graduation, he began a Master's program in plant experimentation and became the first black professor to teach at the school.

But then came the invitation that changed George's life.

Made aware of his agricultural genius, Booker T. Washington, the foremost black educator of the latter part of the nineteenth and early twentieth centuries and president of the Tuskegee Institute, invited George to come and head up the school's agricultural department. George readily accepted. He assured Mr. Washington of his commitment to the position and his overarching long-term vision in education.

"Of course it has always been the one great ideal of my life to be of the greatest good to the greatest number of 'my people' possible," he wrote. "And to this end I have been preparing myself for these many years, feeling as I do that this line of education is the key to unlock the golden door of freedom to our people."[19]

Although grateful for the opportunity, George soon found himself ill-equipped for all the administrative responsibilities expected of him. He wanted to teach and experiment, not manage a stack of papers. After some time and struggle, George was removed from the dry administrative role and put back in the classroom full-time. He couldn't have been happier and wound up serving at the university for forty-seven years.

From his classroom and laboratory at Tuskegee, Carver helped revolutionize the way many farmers planted and harvested their crops. He advocated crop rotation and encouraged the planting of peanuts and soybeans as a means to help return nutrients to the soil. Faced with a potential glut of peanuts and soybeans from his recommendations, George began exploring alternative uses for the abundant crops. From his lab he discovered over 200 uses of the peanut, including in cosmetics and massage oils. He discovered over 100 alternative uses for the sweet potato from candy to flour to paste. George also fulfilled his promise to help black farmers manage their lands more efficiently. Traveling throughout rural areas of Alabama in the Tuskegee Institute Movable School, a large specially equipped wagon, Carver counseled and taught many of the techniques he launched and perfected in his lab.

MORE THAN FARMING

To be sure, George Washington Carver was far more than a brilliant man with a passion for helping people raise healthy and abundant crops. In addition, and perhaps more importantly, he was a man of strong

Christian faith who was committed to helping raise men and women of strong character. At Tuskegee, he taught Sunday school class and was known to say, "When you do the common things in life in an uncommon way, you will command the attention of the world."[20]

When George told a reporter he believed "God is going to reveal [scientific] things to us He never revealed before if we put our hands in His," some of his critics became apoplectic, criticizing him for infusing science with faith.[21] All he was trying to communicate was a belief that one doesn't have to separate their faith from their work, saying that "Without God to draw aside the curtain, I would be helpless."[22]

The *New York Times* published a scathing editorial in which they chided him and said his comments lacked "the scientific spirit."[23] George held his ground. "Inspiration is never at variance with information," he responded, "in fact, the more information one has, the greater will be the inspiration."[24]

Over the years, Carver developed a list of "eight cardinal virtues" for his students to embrace, suggesting they were needed to lead a truly successful life.[25] They were:

- Be clean both inside and out.
- Neither look up to the rich nor down on the poor.
- Lose, if need be, without squealing.
- Win without bragging.
- Always be considerate of women, children, and older people.
- Be too brave to lie.
- Be too generous to cheat.
- Take your share of the world and let others take theirs.

A FINAL WORD

Because he was never interested in notoriety or wealth, when George Washington Carver died on January 5, 1943, his estate held few patents and was worth far less than people of similar stature. On his tombstone was etched the following: "He could have added fortune to fame, but caring for neither, he found happiness and honor being helpful to the world."[26]

Even in death, George Washington Carver was still teaching.

RIDING THE RAILS TO TOMORROW

I t all started with one massive problem and one Christian minister's bold and controversial idea to solve it.

By the 1850s, the streets of New York City were filled with nearly thirty thousand homeless children. They lived in rat-infested cellars or abandoned buildings, inside cardboard boxes, on park benches, and on dirty and dusty street corners—anywhere they could find a place to rest their weary heads. Their predicaments, of course, were due to no fault of their own. Some were abandoned. Some had run away. Others had parents who died of disease or were deemed delinquent and unqualified guardians. Still others came from homes of absolute poverty and were relinquished out of desperation. Perhaps their mouth was one mouth too many for their biological parents to afford to feed.

Regardless of the root cause of their circumstances, they all had one thing in common: they were orphans in need of a home—and the Reverend Charles Loring Brace had a creative solution.

THE INAUGURATION OF THE ORPHAN TRAIN

Aware of Midwestern farms desperately in need of hands and help, why not try and relocate the able-bodied children from the cities to families in the country? There they would find, ideally, loving and nurturing homes in which to be reared. On the farm they would be exposed to fresh air and hard work—all the while contributing to the overall welfare and success of their new families.

To help facilitate such a massive undertaking, Reverend Loring established the Children's Aid Society in 1853. It was headquartered in New York City. There were two different ways Loring and his colleagues attempted to match the orphaned children with their new rural-based families.

The first way, which was somewhat targeted, was to take out advertisements in local Midwestern city newspapers announcing children were available for adoption. Families were invited to contact the Children's Aid Society or New York's Foundling Hospital (which was run by the Catholic Sisters of Charity order) and complete an application including references from a priest or pastor. They were permitted to articulate any specific characteristics they were looking for in the child, from gender to age and even hair and eye color, and overall temperament.

The prospective adoptive couple was required to agree to make sure the adoptee attended school for at least four months of the year, was adequately housed, fed, and clothed, and attended church—to give the child "all the advantages that we would give to a child of our own." The newly arriving family member would be required to stay with their new family until the age of twenty-one. Once a match was made, the child was then put on a train and transported to the station closest to their new family's home.

The second, more popular method of placement was to publish advertisements announcing that between ten and thirty children were on their way via train to a particular city. Prospective adoptive couples were invited to fill out an application and on the day of the train's arrival, evaluate the available children. Arriving in the station, the children were met by a representative of the Children's Aid Society and taken to a nearby theater or opera house. Administrators would line up the children on the stage from tallest to shortest. Prospective parents would then have the opportunity to see and meet them in order to determine if they would be a good fit for their family.

AN IMPERFECT SYSTEM

In later years, the tradition of placing them atop a stage or raised surface (hence the phrase, "put up for adoption") has been derided and likened to the same deplorable methods used during slave auctions. Shaley George, the curator of the National Orphan Train Complex in Concordia, Kansas, while acknowledging the imperfect nature of the process, sees it from a different perspective. "Whoever is up on that stage is the story—he or she is the special person. The goal was not to exploit the children but to provide for them. Charles Loring Brace didn't want the young children to work," she said. "Instead, he wanted them to be placed in a home where they could be prepared to work one day."[1]

Christina Baker Kline, author of the bestselling novel, *Orphan Train*, suggests the newly relocated children were often bluntly and harshly conditioned for their new placement. "They [the children] were told, 'Your parents are not your parents. Your past is not your past. Your life begins when you are chosen.'"[2]

BY THE NUMBERS

In truth, the majority of the 250,000 children who were transported on the "orphan trains" between 1853 and 1929 still had a living family member, often residing back east.[3] In time, some were reunited with one or both of their birthparents, though most never saw them again. In the seventy-six years they were operated, orphan trains visited all forty-eight contiguous states, and some trains even operated from the west coast. It took a while for the orphan train children to realize they were part of a large program, as most just assumed their train was the only one.

Today, officials estimate there are only approximately thirty living members of Reverend Brace's social experiment.

CHAPTER TEN

TOM MONAGHAN

I n the cold twilight of December 24, 1941, just a little over three weeks since the deadly Japanese attack on Pearl Harbor, British Prime Minister Winston Churchill stood alongside President Franklin Roosevelt on the south portico of the White House. Churchill had traveled across the Atlantic to discuss strategy for World War II, which the United States was now fighting with Great Britain both in Europe and across the Pacific.

"This is a strange Christmas Eve," the prime minister said, his distinct accent echoing into the evening air.[1] Thousands were bundled up in front of him, and millions more were tuned in across the country on radio. It was the annual tree lighting ceremony, a traditionally joyous event now somewhat muted and somber due to the ongoing military hostilities.

"Here, in the midst of war, raging and roaring over all the lands and seas, creeping nearer to our hearts and homes, here, amid all the tumult, we have tonight the peace of the spirit in each cottage home and in every generous heart," Churchill continued. "Therefore we may cast aside for this night at least the cares and dangers which beset us, and make for the children an evening of happiness in a world of storm. Here, then, for one night only, each home throughout the English-speaking world should be a brightly-lighted island of happiness and peace. Let the children have their night of fun and laughter. Let the gifts of Father Christmas delight their play. Let us grown-ups share to the full in their unstinted pleasures before we turn again to the stern task and the formidable years that lie before us, resolved that, by our sacrifice and daring, these same children shall not be robbed of their inheritance or denied their right to live in a free and decent world."[2]

Yet, just over five hundred miles to the northwest, in a small A-frame house on Newport Road in Ann Arbor, Michigan, there was neither happiness nor laughter. In fact, four-year-old Thomas Stephen Monaghan was sitting alone by the Christmas tree, confused and scared—trying desperately to make sense of what was going on.

That's because Tom's mother, Anna, was sitting with his father, Frank, at Joseph Mercy Hospital. The twenty-nine-year-old father of two, a tractor-trailer truck driver, was in serious condition. The diagnosis was ulcers and peritonitis, inflammation of the intestines, usually a treatable condition. Sadly, though, Frank's condition was chronic and dire. There would be no cure. By night's end he would be dead.

"When he died, it was very tough," Tom recalled almost seventy years later. "I remember the Christmas tree with a model airplane under it."[3] The days leading up to the funeral became something of a blur for the young boy. Today, he recalls very little of the tragedy but does have a vivid memory concerning the wake at the funeral home.

"MY DAD'S MY HERO"

"Mother took me with her and held my hand as we walked up to the casket," Monaghan remembered. "I was frightened. It didn't seem right for Dad to be lying there. I pulled away from her grip and jumped up on the casket. I grabbed him and hugged him tight, crying, 'Wake up, Daddy! Wake up, Daddy!'"[4]

In the years since his father's passing, Tom Monaghan has regularly lauded his dad, referring to him as "a gentle man" who was "very patient" with him. "I wanted to be with him wherever he went," he said. In Tom's eyes, his father was his "hero" and could do no wrong. Childhood with his dad was a happy time. Despite their modest home, Monaghan says the house "remains in my memory as warm and spacious as a mansion."[5]

EVERYTHING CHANGES

For Thomas Monaghan, Christmas Eve of 1941 marked the beginning of the end of everything predictable and familiar. Anna, Tom's mother, received a $2,000 life insurance payout. She took half of it, paid off their little house, sold the property, and banked the remaining $1,000. Now the sole breadwinner, she landed a job with the Argus Camera Company, earning $27.50 a week.[6] But she found it difficult to manage both Tom and her other son, James. "[She] couldn't see how she could support my brother and me," Tom reflected, perhaps somewhat incredulous but nevertheless understanding. "She'd always had a difficult time managing me. She says that even when I was a baby, before I could walk, which I did at seven months, she couldn't leave me alone for a minute because I was so strong and restless that I'd pull the safety pins right out of my diapers."[7]

The two boys were placed in foster care, moving around a couple of times before landing with Frank and Maria Woppman, a childless, older German couple. The Woppmans were strict and ran a tight ship. Frank was a butcher in a local grocery store and Maria was a housewife. Tom recalls "Uncle Frank," as he called him, would often joke with the boys, but the environment was not overly warm. That the Woppmans didn't attend church struck the young boy as strange. Asking him why, Frank told little Tom, "Just bad people go to church." According to the five-year-old, "I knew he was wrong, even at that age."[8]

In the end, the two boys were too much for the couple to handle and after eighteen months together, it was time to find them a new home.

"PRISON"

From the Woppmans, Tom and James were transferred to St. Joseph's Home for Boys in Jackson, Michigan, a Catholic orphanage run by Felician nuns. According to Tom, the institution was one of two "prisons" in Jackson, the other being the Michigan State Penitentiary.[9] Monaghan resented having to live there but quickly became infatuated with the property's Victorian architecture. He was also introduced to the concept of hard work as each resident was expected to pitch in and help around the property.

"I learned how big that yard was when I had to push one of the dozens of lawnmowers the nuns kept stored behind the latticework of the rambling old porches," he wrote. "I learned a lot of other things in the orphanage too: how to scrub and polish floors and iron shirts and trousers by the hundreds."[10] He was also responsible for keeping the eight-foot-wide grand staircase spotless, regularly dusting and polishing the long banisters.

The development of a good work ethic notwithstanding, Tom was miserable at St. Joseph's and desperately longed for what he had lost; he would often dream his father would somehow, someday return. "I never got over the feeling that my existence was abnormal, that my lot in life was unjust," he said. "I didn't brood about it...I didn't rebel...I only remember feeling intensely unhappy about my strange new surroundings."[11] All residents attended daily Mass, a practice Tom found great comfort in and would eventually return to on his own later in life.

SURROGATE MOTHER

Although Tom's mother Anna was attending a nearby nursing school, the youngster would only see her for occasional visits, mainly on weekends. The separation was difficult. Bitterness and anger began to develop, manifesting itself, among other ways, in the form of a bad temper that often raged red hot. He was angry and confused—and who could blame him? Rescuing him from his own devices was a diminutive Polish nun by the name of Sister Mary Beranda. "She became my surrogate mother, and I flourished under her care," Tom remembered.[12]

Sister Berarda recognized Tom's loneliness and depression and began to pour herself into him, quickly becoming his greatest cheerleader, encouraging him at every turn and infusing him with buckets of self-confidence. Because of Sister Berarda, Tom says, he became "an absolute star at everything" he did. "I was the best jigsaw-puzzle solver, the best Ping-Pong player, the best marble shooter."[13]

The Felician nun also gave him permission to dream, which he often did while walking to school. "Sister Berarda always encouraged me, even when my ideas seemed far-fetched," he said. "I remember telling the class that when I grew up I wanted to be a priest, an architect, and a shortstop for the Detroit Tigers. The other kids laughed and said that was impossible. I couldn't be all three. Sister Berarda quieted them down and said, 'Well, I don't think it's ever been done before, Tommy, but if you want to do it, there's no reason you can't.' That was inspiring."[14]

A NEW HOUSEMOTHER

Unfortunately, Sister Mary was transferred out of St. Joseph's by the time Tom reached the third grade. Her replacement, Sister Ladislaus, was everything Sister Mary Berarda was not. "She ruled by the strap," Tom remembered. "We were whipped for the slightest infraction; there was no leniency, never a reprieve. That housemother was as tough as the strictest drill instructor I ever had in the Marine Corps."[15]

As the years in the orphanage began to accumulate, the Monaghan brothers began to wonder if their mother was ever coming back. By the time Tom reached the sixth grade he assumed she wasn't. Yet, one day, like a bolt out of the blue, she arrived with news she landed a nursing job in Traverse City, and Tom and Jim would be joining her to live in a newly purchased house. "I could hardly believe it," Tom said. "I can recall how exciting it was to be free, to be able to go into stores by myself and look at the merchandise, to be allowed to have money in my pocket, to be able to make money. The transition from the regimentation of the orphanage to complete freedom with my mother was exhilarating."[16]

But it didn't last too long.

"After our years apart," Tom reflected, "it seemed like my mother and I couldn't be together for more than a minute without getting into an argument, so I stayed away from her as much as possible."[17] The sixth grade entrepreneur picked and sold fruit and even peddled fresh fish he caught. But tensions at home continued to rise and Mrs. Monaghan couldn't take it any longer. For the second time in seven years, Tom was placed in foster care.

ON THE ROAD AGAIN

Years later, Tom speculated his mother was likely suffering from some form of mental illness. "She was a good woman," he said. "And I always respected her and liked her enthusiasm, but she had her moments. I remember my mother's tantrums. She might have been a manic depressive. She'd go off without a moment's notice."[18]

But at the time, Anna Monaghan held all the cards and after registering Tom with the state's Children's Home and Aid Society, he took up residence on a succession of family farms. The Johnson family came first, but Tom complained to welfare officials he wasn't getting enough to eat. Opal, his foster care mother, "was not my cup of tea," he said.[19] After six months he was transferred to the Beaman family farm in Interlochen. He especially enjoyed being with Mr. Beaman and liked working with him on the family's gravel truck. For the first time since his father's passing, he had a male role model to emulate.

When Tom enrolled in St. Francis High School back in Traverse City, he moved once more, this time to the farm of Mr. and Mrs. Edwin Crouch. They made a quick and close connection. "I loved them," he said. "They were great people. I work with [Edwin] a lot in the barns. He gave me $2 a week."[20] The Crouchs encouraged Tom to read and dream. "One book I remember reading," Tom wrote, "...was about the boyhood of Abraham Lincoln. His story inspired me to dream big. If a poor farm boy from Illinois could work hard and become president of the United States, why should I put limits on myself?"[21]

CALLED TO MINISTRY

Now a teenager, Tom was beginning to find himself. Walking to the bus stop, he would dream of girls and a career, envisioning himself as an entrepreneurial success or perhaps a master architect following in the footsteps of his childhood hero, Frank Lloyd Wright. A wildly accomplished Tom Monaghan would not just have nice things—he'd have the best things, from houses to cars and everything in between. At the same time, he also became deeply involved at their local Catholic church and found in one of its priests, Father Russell Passeno, a father figure, mentor, and a friend.

"Father Passeno often acted like a real father to me, giving me encouragement and helping smooth out my misunderstandings with my mother," he said.[22] It would be on the Crouch farm, shoveling manure, where Tom first felt the call to the priesthood. "The symbolism of the situation was overpowering: Standing up to my ankles in muck, I saw that I had been wallowing in crass, worldly thoughts when I should have been concentrating on my spiritual quest. I decided then and there that I would become a priest."[23]

Motivated and moved from that moment in the stables, Tom applied to St. Joseph's Seminary in Grand Rapids. The fifteen-year-old began classes in the fall of 1952, just one of the seventy incoming students.

Unfortunately, it didn't go so well.

Although originally thrilled to learn that the headmaster was Monsignor Edmund F. Falicki, a 6'6" former prospect for the New York Yankees, Monaghan quickly found himself back amidst the rigor and order he so despised at the orphanage. Monsignor Falicki's philosophy was to push the young men hard, almost trying to convince them the priesthood wasn't for them. The seminarians, in turn, were to try and convince the rector otherwise. From the beginning, Tom's rebelliousness and frustration with authority got him in trouble. Less than a year after his stint at the seminary began, he was asked to leave.

"I pleaded for another chance," Tom recalled. "I called upon my grades, which were good (except in Greek). I told him [Monsignor

Falicki] about the goals I'd had since I was in the second grade. But he had made up his mind. I was out."[24]

MORE DOMESTIC TROUBLES

Faced with the embarrassing prospect of being kicked out of religious life, Tom slinked back to his mother in Traverse City. "She had thought her problems with me were over when I went off to become a priest," he said. "Now here I was on her doorstep again, and we got right back into our constant bickering."[25]

Now back at St. Francis High School, Tom crawled his way through classes, doing as little as possible to pass. He found a job setting pins at a local bowling alley where he was befriended by yet another surrogate mother. "Marion Conway, who ran the alley with her husband, John, took it on herself to look after me," he said.[26] Marion knew life at home was tough, and so she regularly prepared a hot meal for her employee, often sitting with him and talking over his domestic challenges.

Unfortunately, things went from bad to worse when a County Sheriff apprehended Tom out of the blue one day while he was walking home from school. Tom's mother had labeled her son a juvenile delinquent and arranged for him to be shipped off to a detention home. "I had committed no crime," Tom pleaded. "I had never been delinquent in any way. Yet here I was being locked up like a common thief."[27]

RESCUED

Ashamed and embarrassed to be living under lock and key, Tom kept the news of his detainment from everyone but his high school basketball coach, Joe Kraupa. His fellow housemates were gritty and troubled and the high schooler was forced to protect himself, often resulting in fistfights. Administrators at the home actually depended on Tom to help keep law and order. "They'd ask me to 'Talk to the kid by hand,'" Tom remembered. "I obliged...I frankly enjoyed a good fight."[28]

When Tom's Aunt Peg and Uncle Dan Mahler found out about Tom's plight, they were appalled and made arrangements to bring him to their home in Ann Arbor. It was the best thing that had happened to Tom since December 23, 1941, the day before his father died.

"I was treated like a member of the family and that's what I had craved ever since I first went to the orphanage. I had come close to a family feeling on the farm with Mr. and Mrs. Crouch, but this was really the first time since my mother's death that I felt like I was leading a normal life."[29]

While finally thriving at home, Tom continued to struggle academically. "For some reason I could not buckle down and study," he said. "I barely cracked a book all year. I just played sports and went through the motions in my classes."[30] In the end, though, he made it and graduated, though last in his class. Still harboring a dream of becoming an architect, Tom enrolled at Ferris State College in Big Rapids. It was an architectural trade school with a program that allowed you to test for your licensure after classroom training and nine years of employment.

To pay for his tuition, room, and board, Tom hustled his way through several jobs, including delivering and managing a newspaper distribution outlet and digging ditches for the water company. Given his good grades, he decided to apply to the University of Michigan, but his plans were thwarted when he couldn't find a job in Ann Arbor to help pay for his tuition. Determined to go to college, he enlisted in the U.S. Marines (although he thought it was the Army) after the recruiter told him the government would help him pay his tuition after his military service was up.

MORE CHALLENGES

Life in the United States Marine Corps proved difficult for Tom, but he was determined to make the most of it. "I decided that my hitch in the military would be time completely wasted if I didn't improve my mind as well as my body," he remembered. "So I launched an intensive self-improvement program. I read just about every book in the [Okinawa] base library that I thought might help me, especially inspirational ones, by authors such as Norman Vincent Peale and Dale Carnegie. I also read a lot of biographies and practical books on subjects I thought might be useful to me someday."[31]

As his two-year enlistment in the Marines was winding up, Tom was swindled out of $2,000 in savings by a character that somehow convinced him to invest in an oil well that, as it turned out, didn't even exist. Returning to Ann Arbor and preparing to register at the University of Michigan, the honorably discharged Marine, who was now broke, moved into a two-bedroom apartment with his brother Jim, a full-time mailman. His entrepreneurial juices kicked in again, and Monaghan managed to purchase a newsstand with no money down, a venture that provided him with enough income to make the ends meet. He and his brother also took jobs in a local pizza store run by a gentleman named Dominick DiVarti.

Little did Tom know his part-time job in that pizzeria would plant the seeds that would eventually lead to him revolutionizing the industry and becoming the world's largest and most profitable pizza franchise.

HIS FUTURE IS PIZZA

From that small store in Ann Arbor, Tom learned of a vacant shop owned by his boss Dominick. It was located in the town of Ypsilanti, across from Eastern Michigan University. Would he be willing to let Tom try and make it profitable? Dominick threw Tom the keys. Dominick wanted nothing more to do with it. Tom convinced his brother to help him make a go of the fledgling shop, and before long they were turning a profit. Seeing the potential given its proximity to the school, Tom implemented what would soon become one of his company's signature hallmarks—guaranteed thirty minute delivery. He decided to expand. When Mr. DiVarti balked at his use of "DomiNick's" for a name, Tom searched for another.

"Domino's" was born, eventually growing to over ten thousand corporate and franchise stores in seventy countries. With his newly earned wealth, Tom finally achieved the life he envisioned as a young child bouncing around from the orphanage to multiple foster homes. In 1962 he married Marjorie Zybach, a woman he met while delivering pizza in Ypsilanti. Together they have four daughters—Margaret, Susan, Mary, and Barbara.

LEGACY

In 1983, not content with just the pizza business, he purchased his childhood team, the Detroit Tigers. The next year they won the World Series. Around that same time he established the Mater Christi Foundation, known today as the Ave Maria Foundation, to help fund Catholic media and communication efforts. In 1997, he established Legatus, an organization designed to support and encourage Catholic Fortune 500 CEOs. He has also committed considerable resources to helping preserve the sanctity of every human life.

By the late 1990s, however, Tom still felt spiritually unsettled. Yes, his investments made him a fantastically rich man, but something was just not right. After reading Christian writer and apologist Dinesh D'Souza's, *The Catholic Classics*, Tom identified the source of the problem: his pride.

The truth came to him through the writings of C. S. Lewis. In D'Souza's book, Tom read Lewis's contention, that pride was "the essential vice, the utmost evil...It was through Pride that the devil became the devil. Pride leads to every other vice," Lewis wrote, "it is the complete anti-God state of mind."[32]

"That hit me right between the eyes," Monaghan said. "C. S. Lewis told me that it was pure pride. You want to impress other people— impress them with a spectacular play, or you wanted to impress them with all your worldly goods and accomplishments."[33]

Later that night, Tom Monaghan said he was convinced the Lord was calling him to take a "millionaire's vow of poverty."[34] He went on to sell the Tigers in 1992, and in 1998 he sold 93 percent of the Domino's company to Bain Capital for $1 billion. Since then, the one-time pizza king has been investing the proceeds of his businesses in a wide range of philanthropic causes from a Catholic college and law school to a development north of Naples, Florida, called "Ave Maria Town," a master planned community designed to exemplify and model Christian morals and ideals.

"I had to get rich to see that being rich isn't important," he said. "I was brought up poor and I was embarrassed by my threadbare clothes and shoes. I had to get that out of my system...It was a relief."[35]

ADOPTED BY MANY

Tom Monaghan's corporate ascent and eventual commitment to spreading the Christian gospel was only made possible because of the many surrogate parents in his life. In many ways, each of them adopted him for a season and each one contributed to his sucess. From Sister Mary Berarda to Father Russell Passeno, Mr. and Mrs. Beaman, Coach Joe Kraupa, Opal Crouch, and his aunt and uncle, Peggy and Dan Mahler, Thomas Monaghan's world was changed because so many were willing to temporarily change theirs.

CHAPTER ELEVEN

NEWT GINGRICH

When you consider the circumstances surrounding the birth and subsequent adoption of Newt Gingrich, it seems fitting he arrived in the midst of the Second World War.

He was born "Newton Leroy McPherson" on June 17, 1943. Strong thunderstorms with warm rain rattled the Pennsylvania town of Harrisburg that day. His mother, Kathleen "Kit" Daugherty, had married his biological father, Newt, just a year earlier. They met at a roller rink after Kit quit high school to clean houses, trying to help her family following the tragic death of her father, who worked on the railroad and was killed in a car accident.

"I wanted to break our engagement and my mother said, 'You can't because it's going to be in the paper tomorrow.' My mother made me go through with the wedding," she told the columnist Gail Sheehy. "I didn't want anyone to come."[1] Later, reflecting on the incident, she said, "I never should have gotten married, but I didn't have anyone. I know now I did," she acknowledges, "but at the time, I didn't know because my aunt, my mother's sister—I should have gone to her. She would have backed me up...but then we wouldn't have Newtie, you know, so—I'd rather have him."[2]

Kit's new husband, Newt's father, was also named Newt and known for an explosive temper and complicated personality. He abused her just two days after the wedding, hitting Kit when she tried to cajole him out of bed for work. He had been drinking heavily the night before and was likely nursing a major hangover. "We were married on a Saturday and I left on a Tuesday," she said. "I got Newtie in those three days."[3]

"My [biological] father grew up as a very angry person," Newt reflected. "When he signed up for the Navy, the recruiting officer said, 'Why did you fill out your application wrong?' He said, 'What do you mean?' And he said, 'You put your grandmother's name in where your mother's name should be.' He found out that he had been born out of wedlock. They never told him. Talk about being outraged!"[4]

As it was, the story of Newt's biological father's childhood reads like a dysfunctional Hollywood saga. Only it's not fiction, but cold, hard fact. Newt Senior's biological father was a man named Robert Kersetter, who abandoned him at birth. The little baby was taken in by Newton and Hattie McPherson and everyone was told—including Newt himself—that the boy's biological mother, Louise Kepner, was his sister.

According to the former Speaker of the House and now popular conservative author and historian, "Big Newt was physically enormous. Six foot three, and could use a nine-pound sledgehammer with one hand. I'd say from the time he was sixteen to thirty-five he was in bar fights.... My mother was very frightened of him. So she decides to file for divorce. He tries to talk her out of it, fails, scares her even more, so she divorces him."[5]

LIFE AS A SINGLE MOM

Completely out of options after "Big Newt" shipped off with the Merchant Marine, Newt's mother filed divorce papers with Harrisburg County and moved with the baby back in with her mother, a schoolteacher, who lived nearby. Little Newt became the center of attention and was lavishly doted on by relatives in the area. It wasn't long, though, before Kit needed to find work, which she did as a "junior mechanic" at a local factory supplying goods for the war effort. During the day the infant was cared for by a host of relatives, but primarily his grandmother, Ethel Daugherty, along with his aunt and uncle, Calvin and Loma Troutman.

"They lived in the country, and I loved playing and walking around their land," Newt remembered wistfully. The virtues of dedicated commitment and personal responsibility were drilled into the youngster on a daily basis. "Uncle Cal worked very hard at building roads. Their own lives had been improved by constant hard work. They simply took it for granted that was the way life was, having grown up in very demanding times: if they did not cut wood, there would be no fire in the cast-iron stove; if they did not can food, there would be slim pickings in midwinter and their diet would suffer. The result was a focus on daily, steady work, an ethic they passed on to me and that has stayed with me to this day."[6]

In fact, qualifying Calvin Troutman as "tough" doesn't even tell the half of it. According to Newt, while his Uncle Cal was on the job one day, he was shot and chased the guy—but, "He couldn't catch him because of the bullet in his leg."[7]

REMARRIAGE

One night, with the war winding down, Kit found herself again at the local roller rink. There she met a young Army officer. His name was Robert Gingrich. He was the strong, silent type. They began talking and hit it off. That fateful meeting served as the turning point in not only her life, but in the life of her two-year-old son. Within the year they married, an instant family of three.

A Pennsylvania native, Robert Gingrich was thirty years old and prior to becoming an artillery officer in the Army, worked on the Reading Railroad. After marrying Newt's mother, the family moved to an apartment above an Esso gas station in Hummelstown, Pennsylvania, a small town located nine miles east of the state capital of Harrisburg. There at the corner of Main and Hanover Streets the Gingrichs settled into their new lives.

For a young boy, Hummelstown was an idyllic, small-town setting that enabled Newt to dream and explore. Along with his younger sisters, Susan (born in 1948) and Roberta (1950), the Gingrich trio enjoyed the historic but rural simplicity of the area. During a visit to his old hometown in the midst of the 2012 presidential campaign, Newt reminisced about wandering through the local rock quarry and hiking "through the swamp" to Hershey. "When you were 8 or 9 or 10 years old these were great adventures. This was like going to Africa."[8] In fact, Edward Schwartz, a boyhood friend of Newt's, recalled the richness of his friend's imagination, which was stoked by his surroundings. "I remember the first time I ever met him he was 4 years old," he said. "He was coming down the alley in one of those African helmets."[9] As boys, Schwartz and Gingrich played together at Echo Caverns, a limestone cave that's a tourist attraction today.

TURNING POINT

The movies proved to be a great source of inspiration for Newt. For special treats his mom or dad would take him to downtown Harrisburg to the Loews Theater for the Saturday matinees. He was particularly drawn to animal films, and at the age of ten, having just watched one and inspired with an idea, he walked from the theater to City Hall. He told his parents he was going to the library, but there he was opining that he thought the town should reopen a zoo closed during World War II. The mayor's office was taken with the polite but precocious boy. After inviting him to plead his case before the city council at their next meeting, the mayor introduced him to a gentleman named Paul Walker who worked at the *Harrisburg Home Star*, the city's largest newspaper.

Newt's testimony at the city council became front page news. "Young Newton Gingrich told Mayor Claude Robins and four city councilmen that he and a number of youthful buddies could round up enough animals to get the project started," read the Associated Press account in 1954.[10] His appreciation for wildlife would be a lifelong passion. As a member of the House of Representatives, he supported the Endangered Species Act, a hot-button piece of legislation many of his fellow conservatives opposed. More recently, he's spoken eloquently and forcefully about a Christian's responsibility to manage the earth's resources.

Mayor Robins's introduction of Paul Walker to Newt proved to be a providential encounter. Walker, impressed with Gingrich's fierce curiosity coupled with his ability to listen, encouraged the young boy to read *Walden* and *Civil Disobedience* by Henry David Thoreau. Walker invited Newt to hang out at the newspaper office, which he wound up doing on a regular basis. He took ads, answered phones, and most importantly, soaked up the writing environment. Newt's grandmother and aunt had already planted in him a love of books, but here he was physically immersed and surrounded by ideas and words. He loved every minute of it.

Paul Walker also introduced Newt to Frank Canton, a conservative writer and radio news director in Pennsylvania who further fed Newt's intellectual appetite. At WHP, Newt was given the opportunity to interview newsmakers on the radio and read commentaries. He was beginning to hone his craft of persuasive communication. Newt tagged along with Paul and Frank to meetings attended by local attorneys and politicians. The boy mostly listened, but according to Paul, when he did speak up, he "quietly expressed" himself in a "very gentlemanly" manner. "He was practical," Paul added, always "...trying to find the truth."[11]

THE IMPACT OF HOLLYWOOD

Adventurous, dramatic, and historic films also played an important role in the development of Newt's worldview, specifically the belief freedom and liberty were fragile and demanded careful attention. He would later say there was "a moment [during the movies] where I realized, I can be a leader."[12] He loved it when good guys like Jimmy Stewart and Gary Cooper won on the big screen. The films may have been fictitious, but the principles and values they communicated were valid and important. Young Newt was drawn to the grittiness and toughness of certain characters.

When he was nine, he broke his arm trying to imitate Burt Lancaster swinging up to a tree limb. He also loved the Duke. "I imprinted John Wayne as my model of behavior," he once told a reporter. "I was a 50-year-old at 9."[13] The movies, always the great cultural magnifier, helped to reinforce what Newt's adoptive father and uncle were already modeling: American manhood was serious business and a responsibility every good male citizen should embrace.

FROM MCPHERSON TO GINGRICH

Given that Kit and Bob married when Newt was just three, it never occurred to the youngster that Robert Gingrich wasn't his biological father. After all, it would be rare for a three-year-old to have memories of a wedding or life as a two-year-old without a father. But behind the scenes and obviously unbeknownst to Newt, his biological father called Kit shortly after she married Bob with an unusual offer.

"His new wife was pregnant," she remembered. "He [Big Newt] said that if I would drop the past four months of child-support payments, Bob could adopt Newtie."[14] (The law requires living biological parents to relinquish parental rights before permitting an individual to be adopted.)

The Gingrichs readily agreed, and Newt's adoption was finalized by the end of 1946.

A WINDOW TO THE WIDER WORLD

By 1951, with the war in Korea heating up, Bob Gingrich was deployed to East Asia. Kit remained in Hummelstown with their eight-, three-, and one-year-olds. Over thirty-six thousand American lives were lost in the three year conflict, but to the Gingrich family's relief, Bob returned safely in 1953. But change was in the air. After having spent the first eleven years of his life in Pennsylvania, Newt was moving to Fort Riley in Kansas.

The one-hundred-thousand-acre Army base in north central Kansas further fed the ten-year-old's curiosity. He considered the move to be a big break. Grateful to have his father back from the war, the family of five moved into modern modular housing. Newt was enthralled with the environment and would wander the base, climbing on tanks used for rifle-grenade practice. "It was a great adventure," Newt would later say.[15]

At Fort Riley, Newt's parents bought him his first dog, a Doberman Pinscher. He named him "Captain's Pride of Riley," and the two quickly became inseparable. So strong was Gingrich's devotion to the dog that once when "Pride" fell though the ice of a nearby pond, twelve-year-old Newt jumped in after him. Rescuers had to pull both of them to safety. The experience left a big impression on the young boy. He said being trapped under the ice would teach him the importance of remaining calm in the midst of a crisis. "I learned not to panic."[16]

It was also at Fort Riley that an intelligence commanding officer, Colonel Lucias Clay, took a special interest in Newt, recognizing the youth's quick mind and leadership potential. The two of them talked informally about war, peace, and politics. He suggested books to him and took time to listen and critique Newt's ideas and developing worldview.

OFF TO EUROPE

By 1957 the Gingrichs were on the move again, this time relocating with the Army to Orleans, France. For his eighth and ninth grade years, the family crammed into a one bedroom hotel room. It was a far cry from Harrisburg and Fort Riley, but he loved it. They eventually rented the first floor of a chateau in the quaint town of Beaugency, which was located downriver from the base.

Much to Newt's delight, the family ventured around Europe during the summer months. He attended the bullfights in Barcelona, Spain, and the Brussels World's Fair. With the escalation of the Cold War, he was particularly intrigued with the Soviet Union pavilion. "I must have collected 600 pamphlets there to take home and study the next few weeks," he said.[17] A ten-speed bicycle allowed him to explore both the countryside and nearby towns. That Christmas his father gave him an entire set of encyclopedias. The more he read, the more he wanted to read.

TURNING POINT

The penny really dropped, however, during a visit to the French town of Verdun. The Battle of Verdun in World War I between France and Germany lasted 303 days and cost a record 305,000 lives between both countries. Evidence of the wartime devastation was still evident everywhere he turned.

The Gingrich's had come to see Darvin and Sue Patrick, old Army friends from Harrisburg. Darvin was a prisoner in a Japanese camp during WWII, and so their house was filled with the type of memorabilia Newt had never seen. They visited various battlefields and on the way back stopped in a museum. With the tourist building was an ossuary—a site reserved for human remains. The door was locked, but Newt could see through the window and he couldn't believe what he saw—bones from thousands upon thousands of war dead from the Battle of Verdun.

"That last day [in Verdun] was probably the most stunning event of my life," Newt would later say. "It was a sense of coming face to face with an unavoidable reality."[18] For Gingrich that reality was that war was evil and brutal and that man had to find another way to settle differences. From that day forward, despite their obvious ideological differences, Newt would often quote the Chinese dictator Mao Zedong who once observed that "War is politics with blood; politics is war without blood."[19]

And so it was in Verdun, France, Newt began to pull all the pieces of his life's calling together. If the men and movies in his life showed him how to act, the horrors of war reminded him of the virtues and grand possibilities of deft political leadership and why combat should always be the act of last resort.

The next day he reportedly told friends and family he would one day run for Congress and help make sure history wouldn't repeat itself. "People like me," he said, "are what stand between us and Auschwitz."[20]

ANOTHER LESSON

By the summer of 1958, the Gingrichs were transferred to Stuttgart, Germany. The family's arrival on July 15, 1958, just happened to coincide with President Eisenhower's launching of "Operation Blue Bat" that very same day. With the promise to intervene globally if the United States feared a regime was being threatened by communism, Newt remembers his father talking about an ever present danger. He shared with the family the "vividness of the reality of the Cold War and of the immense potential combat that was absolutely part of the world."[21]

Within three months the tensions were quelled by diplomacy, but what Newt witnessed in Stuttgart would make a lasting impression. "When you are awakened at 3:00 A.M. by an alert and watch your dad and the 7th Army HQ go into the field, there is a real sense that you are a hostage in a way," Gingrich would later reflect.

Now a full-fledged "Army brat" teenager in Germany, Newt found work in between his studies setting pins at the base bowling alley and working at the library on the post. Those jobs were mundane but everything around him was firing up his senses. He was grateful to his father for a career that allowed him to enjoy history up close and personal. It was one thing to read in books about what happened but a whole other thing to see evidence of history first-hand.

Newt and his Army friends, or often just Newt, explored their surroundings whenever possible. "The world is large, interesting, and constantly changing and full of amazing things," he once said. "Why wouldn't you be sort of happy and amused and wander around learning when given the opportunity?"[22]

BOMBSHELL

It was in the middle of all these good things Newt learned the secret his parents had been keeping from him since 1946. The news about his adoption hit him hard. He had all kinds of questions, especially why his biological father was willing to "sell" his birth name away. His parents did their best to answer each one of the questions, but the sting still stuck.

Faced with such news, how does a teenager avoid the temptation to feed their bitterness? First, he began to fantasize his birth father was a conquering hero in the Merchant Marine and would reclaim him upon the Gingrichs' return to the United States. Naturally, neither was true. When "Big Newt" was released from the service with a punctured eardrum, he went to work as a railroad engineer and then a bread truck driver. It was honest work, but it was also unremarkable. Adding insult to injury, when Newt reached out to him, he didn't want to have anything to do with him.

Exacerbating everything was the fact Newt struggled from time to time navigating his highly disciplined, rules-oriented adoptive father. Bob Gingrich, who died of lung cancer in 1996 at the age of seventy-one, was classic old-school military. "Some people thought I was too rough with Newt," he once told an interviewer. "I just wanted him to get out of the house and earn a living."[23] By his own admission, though, he wasn't the touchy-feely type dad. He never hugged his son. "You don't do that with boys," he said shortly before his death, "I didn't even do it with my girls."[24]

Yet, the love between father and son was on full display at the time of Bob's death, which happened just hours before his son was reelected Speaker of the House. After all, it was Bob Gingrich's career that opened doors to Newt that would have otherwise been closed. Upon learning of his father's passing on November 20, 1996, Gingrich said his father believed "Duty, honor, country were more than words. They were a way of life."[25]

THE COURSE IS SET

The advantage of time allows us to compare and contrast a young Newt's ideals and dreams with today's reality. How did he fare in the pursuit of his largest goals? Of course, we now know Newt Gingrich represented Georgia's 6th congressional district between 1979 and 1999. He led what became known as the "Republic Revolution," that began with his upset election to the role of Speaker of the House in 1994, a role no Republican held in the previous forty years. "I'm a little like the kid who wanted a pony, and now I have this entire back-yard full of ponies and somebody's already told me that you've got to feed them and clean them, and you've got to worry about it," he said at the time.[26] "And I'm excited by the opportunity, but on the other hand, boy is it a lot of work."[27]

In his role as Speaker, he was the co-author and architect of the "Contract with America," a pledge to reform welfare, balance the budget, and cut taxes, among other things. Under his leadership, Congress accomplished all three, and he was named *Time* magazine's "Man of the Year" in 1995. His tenure as Speaker was also marked by significant acrimony, including a government shutdown and charges of ethics violations, largely partisan in nature.

For all the professional highs in his long career of government service, Newt Gingrich has suffered numerous personal low points. Two failed marriages and a highly publicized resignation in 1999 served to humble the brash boy from Harrisburg.

"There's no question at times in my life, partially driven by how passionately I felt about this country, that I worked too hard and things happened in my life that were not appropriate," he once acknowledged.[28]

Today, Newt Gingrich continues to try and shape public policy by advocating and championing the same ideals that drove him as a ten-year-old from a dark movie theater to the steps of city hall.

CHAPTER TWELVE

SCOTT HAMILTON

Horatio Alger couldn't have scripted it any better.

On February 13, 1980, with a stiff, cold breeze blowing off Lake Placid's Whiteface Mountain, twenty-one-year-old figure skater Scott Hamilton slowly led his team into the snow-covered horse show grounds for the opening ceremony of the 13th Winter Olympic games. Trumpets blared. Drums rolled. The colors of eighty countries circled the arena. Elected by his teammates to carry the American flag, the 5'3" Ohio native carefully steadied the stars and stripes in the leather harness strapped across his chest.

"If I start to fly away, will somebody please grab me?" he shouted, half-jokingly, to no one in particular.[1]

"As we began the march through the stadium gates, my hat was practically covering my eyes," he remembered, adding, "not a good thing for the guy leading the hundred member American team."[2]

The next day, the *Washington Post* described him as an "Olympic nobody—just a fellow who finished a respectable third in the U.S. Olympic trials in men's singles."[3]

Of course, that "Olympic nobody" would eventually go on to become a highly accomplished and decorated "Olympic somebody" who took home a gold medal in 1984 and went on to win, among other honors, four consecutive U.S. and World Championships.

The story behind his selection to carry the flag in 1980 and his inspirational career as an athlete, broadcaster, husband, father, and cancer awareness activist is a colorful combination of Providence and persistence culminating in both tragedy and triumph. Its details seem to be almost straight out of central casting.

THE BEGINNING

Scott Scovell Hamilton was born on August 28, 1958, in Toledo, Ohio. His vital statistics at birth would serve to foreshadow his petiteness as an adult—just five pounds, seven ounces, and nineteen-and-a-half inches long.

Nothing is known about his birth parents. Was his biological mother young and unwed? Was his biological father aware of his birth? Would they somehow anonymously track him throughout his life, read about him in the newspapers, watch his athletic exploits on television? We just don't know.

What we do know, however, is Scott was placed in the protective care of Lucas County Child and Family Services sometime between his birth and the beginning of October of 1958. It would be from that agency his parents, Dorothy and Ernest Hamilton, would adopt him at just six weeks of age.

When the Hamiltons arrived in Toledo on that fall day to receive their newborn son, they brought with them Susan, their five-year-old biological daughter. Hope, excitement, and anticipation were running high. In the years since Susan's birth in 1953, Dorothy and Ernie had lost three children—two of them to miscarriage and one, a boy named Ernest Everett, just eight hours after birth. Crestfallen and desiring siblings for Susan, the Hamiltons were thrilled to be adopting Scott. At long last, their prayers were answered. Their dream came true.

At the time of Scott's birth, the Hamiltons were living in a rented three-bedroom tract home on State Street in Bowling Green, Ohio, where Ernest taught botany at the university. Dorothy was an elementary school teacher. The Hamilton side of the family hailed from the Revolutionary war hero and first treasurer of the United States, Alexander Hamilton. Dorothy's family claimed ancestral linkage to John Adams, the second president of the United States.

But in the fall of 1958, all that mattered to the newly formed family of four was that the heirloom family crib built by Scott's maternal grandfather was now holding their newborn son.

UNIVERSITY TOWN LIFE

By Scott's memory, life for a young boy in the college town of Bowling Green was idyllic. Nicknamed "Scooter" because he was constantly in motion, the toddler recalls lush, tree-lined streets and plenty of parks in which to play. "The neighborhood was filled with kids, many of them sons and daughters of other professors at the university," Scott recalled. "The dominant plant in town was a ketchup factory, and when the wind was blowing just right, there was no escaping the scent of cooking tomatoes. But what made this community special was the university. It drew people from other cultures who otherwise never would have set foot in Bowling Green. And my parents got to know these kids because my father served as an academic advisor for foreign exchange students."[4]

Exposure to such diversity in an otherwise white town helped to do more than impress upon the little boy a spirit of justice and equality. In addition, it trained Scott to openly and comfortably communicate with people of different races, a skill that would greatly benefit him as an international skater and later as a television commentator. Jim Karugo was one student who regularly visited the house. Scott was enamored with the Kenyan's ability to play the drums and in return, the student taught the Hamilton children basic Swahili.

HEALTH CHALLENGES MOUNT

In 1962, Dorothy and Ernest adopted a second boy, Steven. Thrilled to welcome home a third child, the Hamiltons' exuberance was somewhat muted when four-year-old Scott began struggling with a series of upper respiratory ailments. "I was getting sick all the time," he remembered. "While I was eating plenty at mealtime, my parents noticed I was having trouble digesting my food and was severely constipated. My ribs showed and my abdomen was noticeably distended. Most alarming was that it appeared I had stopped growing."[5]

Visits to various specialists began to pile up. Months of mystery turned to years. All the tests were inconclusive with most physicians labeling it malabsorption syndrome. Later tests suggested he was allergic to dairy and gluten. Yet another pointed toward Cystic Fibrosis. The Hamiltons dutifully followed doctor's instructions, adjusting Scott's diet based on the latest diagnosis.

At Children's Hospital in Boston, Dorothy and Scott were introduced to Dr. Henry Shwachman, a professor at Harvard Medical School who specialized in cystic fibrosis and gastrointestinal disorders. Doctor and patient immediately hit it off. After four days of examinations and testing, Dr. Shwachman announced that he suspected Scott was suffering from a pancreatic enzyme deficiency—a disorder that Henry Shwachman had discovered years earlier. But since he couldn't confirm the diagnosis, he urged Dorothy to take Scott home and let him live as normally as possible.

If there was a silver lining to the marathon of tests, it was that through it all, Scott grew increasingly close to his mother. "From these experiences an unshakable bond formed between us," he reflected. "She became my tireless medical advocate."[6]

Dorothy Hamilton's perseverance with her son's medical challenges would be tested in the coming years. After a doctor told Mrs. Hamilton her son had less than six months to live unless he started gaining weight, a feeding tube was inserted into his nose. Scott grudgingly went along with the treatment, though he worried about enduring the ridicule of fellow students. Thankfully, he had garnered the respect of the toughest kid in class, Abel Trevino.

"Abel had long hair, a muscular build and a reputation among the kids that preceded him," Scott once wrote. "Sometimes he appeared out of nowhere like a comic book superhero to bail me out."[7]

A LESSON IN HUMILITY

As the smallest kid in class and managing significant special needs, Scott became accustomed to being different. And while he usually handled the extra attention in stride, his maturity didn't come overnight. As part of his treatment, he was allowed to drink a can of Coke each day to help boost his energy. On one particular day, when he was in the third grade, he chugged the soda quickly and proceeded to let out a loud belch. His fellow students loved it. His teacher, Diane Hunter, did not.

"She took me in the hallway and chewed me out," Scott remembered. "'That's disgusting,' she said. 'You probably think you're really cute because you're getting all this attention for something gross like that.'"[8]

"I was speechless, yet she taught me a good lesson," he said. "Just because I was sickly didn't mean I was exempt from the rules. I was upset with Mrs. Hunter that day, but years later I can appreciate the fact she didn't cut me any slack. I was acting like a pampered kid and she showed me I had to stay on the same page as the rest of the class."[9]

INTRODUCTION TO HIS FUTURE

It was in the midst of Scott's mysterious ailment he was invited on an outing to the new ice skating rink at Bowling Green University—a day that would for him shape every day thereafter. And his mother almost didn't let him go.

Dr. Andrew Klepner was a relatively new arrival to Bowling Green. He had become not only the Hamiltons' physician but also a good family friend. When he arrived at the house one day to take Susan with their family skating, he proposed taking eight-year-old Scott along. His mother refused. Scott's first foray on skates four years earlier on an icy driveway did not go very well. Attempting to balance himself on double-bladed skates, Scott fell backward and badly banged his head.

"Just let him go," Dr. Klepner urged. "There are three people there to keep an eye on him."[10]

Dorothy Hamilton finally relented, and in an instant the door to Scott Hamilton's future swung wide open.

"When we arrived at the rink, I ran ahead and burst through the doors," Scott remembers. "Skating was a struggle at first. I clung to the boards and stayed close to Sue. I had a few more bad spills and there were tears, but I didn't quit. For once I was on even footing with everyone else."[11]

GOOD THINGS BEGIN TO HAPPEN

After just one public session of skating with the Klepners, Scott couldn't get enough of his newfound sport. He regularly badgered his mother to take him to the ice arena, which she did on a weekly basis. Soon, though, once a week wasn't enough to satisfy him. "With each trip to the rink, my parents noticed my mood would brighten considerably," Scott said. "My coordination and close proximity to the ice gave me an advantage."[12]

Recognizing their son's natural ability on skates, the Hamiltons signed Scott up for a group lesson each Saturday with a woman named Rita Lowery. Rita and her husband, David, were a retired champion Canadian figure skater pair who had been recruited by Bowling Green University to set up both a skating and hockey program for the school. But Scott quickly outgrew the group lesson and convinced his parents to arrange for private lessons with Rita. Soon, the nine-year-old was skating in competitions.

Best of all, Scott discovered the more he skated the better he felt and the more energy he seemed to possess. By the time he turned ten, almost all of the symptoms of his mysterious malabsorption syndrome had disappeared.

"Nobody could say for sure what prompted the change in my health and attitude, but my mother speculated that skating had something to do with it. She noticed that the cold, damp air at the ice rink helped my breathing, and the more I skated, the more confident I got."[13]

STRAINS OF SUCCESS

Despite all the good that was happening in the young skater's life, the reality of Scott's newly developed talent began to take its toll on the Hamilton family. It's rarely easy for parents to manage budding athletic talent in a child, especially in a sport like figure skating.

There's the ego, of course, but there's also a host of other challenges associated with raising a prodigy. The demanding practice schedules usually require mom or dad to rise in the pre-dawn dark and shuttle the athlete to and from workouts. Diets must be monitored. Competitions often require travel and a constant juggling of priorities. Then there's the cost of it all.

As teachers, Ernie and Dorothy made very modest salaries. At one point, the costs associated with Scott's skating exploits ($8,000) accounted for half of the family's yearly income. In later years, Ernie leveraged the equity in the house to help finance Scott's training, nearly putting the family on the brink of bankruptcy.

Sibling jealousy also reared its ugly head. Scott's sister, Susan, was beginning to grow weary of all the attention paid to her brother. "Everything's Scotty, Scotty, Scotty," she would regularly lament.[14]

"Watching my parents' lives orbit around mine was frustrating to her," Scott said. "For the first nine years of my life, it was because I was sick most of the time. Then my skating took over."[15]

At home, Scott's brother, Steve, also wound up shouldering a double share of chores. With his brother consumed with his training, the responsibility of mowing the lawn and shoveling the snow fell on Steve. Although he never complained, Scott always sensed Steve harbored some resentment toward him.

MOVING UP AND MOVING OUT

By the time Scott turned thirteen, his parents determined if their son was going to take his skating to the next level, he was going to have to find more sophisticated coaching than was available in the Bowling Green community. Friends of the family suggested the Wagon Wheel training center in Rockton, Illinois. There Scott would meet Slavka

Kohout and Pierre Brunet, internationally acclaimed coaches who helped train Olympic skaters.

Signing up at the Wagon Wheel facility would require the teenager to leave home, a prospect that didn't seem to faze him. "I knew I wanted to keep skating, and that was the most important thing in my life," he said. "I was excited about the possibility of training there, even though it would be tough on my folks. I didn't mind leaving home if it meant I could skate more. I had no idea where skating was going to take me; all I knew was I didn't want to stop."[16]

Scott's time at Wagon Wheel proved crucial in his skating development, but it also exposed the thirteen-year-old to the rowdy, irreverent, and rebellious behavior of his eighteen-year-old roommates. "Good thing she [my mom] didn't know half of what was going on," Scott recalled. "A half-hour drive away was the Wisconsin state line and with it, a legal drinking age of eighteen. I spent a lot of nights alone at the dorm. While my roommates were out barhopping, I was the designated fibber who covered for them during room check. Sometimes they returned totally smashed."[17]

On the ice, Scott's instructor, Olympic coach Pierre Brunet, pushed Scott and his fellow students hard. If they fell in the middle of a routine, they were instructed to start all over. Compassion and empathy were foreign concepts to those in leadership. The kids were there to learn—and learning was hard work. If their parents were willing to pay a steep financial price for their instruction, the skaters were expected to buckle down and toughen up.

A SEASON OF SORROW AND GRIEF

Years of financial struggle finally came to a head in 1975 when Scott's parents announced they could pay for just one year more of instruction. Dorothy Hamilton was diagnosed with breast cancer, forcing her to resign her teaching position. "I loved to skate, but I agreed it made perfect sense," Scott said. "My mom took priority."[18]

Perhaps relieved of the pressures associated with high expectation, Scott began to skate with a renewed sense of purpose, and his coaches took notice.

He began to land jumps previously evasive to him. While the prospect of giving up his dream of one day becoming a championship skater somewhat saddened him, the seventeen-year-old became philosophical about it all. He was given a great gift and gave it a good shot. He could return to Bowling Green, earn his degree and teach skating at the university. After all, it was just a sport. Juxtaposed with what he was witnessing with his mother's illness, skating was a fun life—but it wasn't a matter of life or death.

Unfortunately, Dorothy's health deteriorated rapidly. Scott returned to Bowling Green as often as possible, fearing each time he saw her could be the last visit. In the midst of his mother's decline, the Hamiltons' friend and family doctor—Andrew Klepner—the man who encouraged Dorothy to allow Scott to skate—died of cancer. Sorrow seemed to be surrounding the youngster.

ADOPTION CURIOSITY

During his second-to-last visit before her death, Scott decided to ask his mother about his birth parents, something he had never before broached. He had recently been talking with a friend who was adopted and who was searching for his birth parents. In addition, all the unexpected illness surrounding him, coupled with his own medically checkered past, got him thinking about what he may have genetically inherited from his biological mother and father.

"Mom, can I ask something?" he said.

"Sure," she replied.

"I wonder who my birth parents are?"

By the look on his mother's face, he knew he had managed to wound her with the innocent and completely reasonable question.

"Is there something we've done?" she replied. "Have Dad and I let you down in any way?" she asked softly. "We've tried to give you everything," she continued. "We love you and have sacrificed for you."[19]

Scott would later say he immediately regretted bringing it up.

"I know, Mom. I'm sorry," he quickly answered. "I didn't mean anything by it."[20]

"Can I tell you what I think makes someone a parent?" Dorothy went on. "It's the person who changes a child's diapers, feeds him; takes him to school; helps him with his homework; hugs him when he cries and offers advice and perspective. A parent is there to hold a child when he needs stitches and washes his hands when they're dirty. A parent is someone who is there for a child every day."[21]

DEATH AND LEGACY

Dorothy Hamilton died just weeks later on May 19, 1977. The loss, though expected, devastated Scott. He walked around in a daze for several days. She was his closest friend and cheerleader. The prospect of life without her seemed nearly inconceivable.

"She showed me how to reach for something extra when the logical decision is to give up," he remembered. "Most of all, she taught me to take responsibility for my ability. My mother had worked hard and suffered much to keep me in skating. It was an awful burden to put on myself, but a part of me felt her death would be in vain if I didn't accomplish something in the sport. She had an unwavering faith in my talent and my ability, more than I did at that time. Only after she died did I start believing in myself."[22]

A RENEWED SPIRIT

Dorothy Hamilton's death did, indeed, seem to light a fire under Scott. Later that same year he placed third at the Chicago Midwesterns and qualified for the world championships in Ottawa. After years of skating in anonymity, Scott was now on people's radars. He was beginning to challenge the favorites. More medals at various events followed. In 1980, Scott qualified for the United States Olympic team, placing fifth overall. In 1984 he capped his amateur career by winning the gold medal at the Winter Games in Sarajevo.

Making good on a promise he made to his dying wife, Scott's father, Ernie, was in the stands for every major competition.

After he secured the gold medal, Scott skated a victory lap around the rink of Zetra Olympic Hall, carrying the American flag high above his head. As he did, his mind wandered back to the many challenges of his childhood in Bowling Green and the prediction his mother repeatedly made to family and friends. "Someday Scotty is going to be in the Olympics," she would say.[23] The bold prediction embarrassed him back then. Now it brought tears to his eyes.

"I carried her memory with me each step of the way and it pushed me forward," Scott says. "Now that I'm a little older than my mother was, I deal with the loss of every person who has crossed my path by living for them. I bring the love I had for them with me every single day."[24]

MAKING A LIVING

In the late spring, after a wildly busy few months following the 1984 Winter Olympics, including numerous media interviews and a trip to the White House to meet President Reagan, Scott retired from amateur skating. The timing was right. A new crop of younger skaters was emerging and the twenty-six-year-old was eager to end on a high note. He officially concluded his amateur status by participating in a show to raise money for cancer research, a poignant and fitting move given the death of his mother to the disease just seven years earlier.

In May of 1984, Scott signed a multi-year deal with the Ice Capades, a traveling group of skaters, many of whom were former Olympians. The money was good, and he was finally able to give back to the many people who helped him along the way. He bought a Ford Crown Victoria for his dad along with a two-bedroom house in Lake Placid, Florida. When his father resisted, Scott told him, "You suffered, you gave and you sacrificed. It would make me feel a whole lot better if you accepted this from me." Ernie agreed.[25]

After seventeen years of intense competition, Scott welcomed the change of pace. "I guess what I look forward to is not having to worry about winning or losing or anything else," he said. "I just want to skate well."[26]

The intensity of it all had taken its toll. Winning the gold medal came at a price. In the later years, Scott suffered from stomach ulcers and felt like the stress and strain contributed to his hair loss. At the same time, he became somewhat addicted to fame and status. Reflecting on the new rhythm of professional skating, Scott once said, "But I will miss getting a new title each year. New Year's Eve is the worst night of my life, because New Year's Day I don't have my title anymore. I feel kind of naked. So each year on New Year's Eve, I sulk."[27]

MORE CHALLENGES

In 1986 Scott left the Ice Capades and created his own company called "Scott Hamilton's American Tour," later renamed "Stars on Ice." Professionally, his career was thriving. He began to also take on work as a television commentator and became a popular speaker around the country.

In early 1997, after struggling through months of abdominal discomfort and pain, the thirty-nine-year-old skater drove himself to an emergency room in Peoria, Illinois. After finding a mass in his abdomen, he was referred to the Cleveland Clinic, where he was diagnosed with testicular cancer. He immediately began chemotherapy, which reduced the grapefruit-sized tumor down to a golf ball–sized mass. Surgery followed. After a five month recuperation period, Scott was back out on the ice. In his spare time, he began encouraging people, especially stubborn men, to get regular physicals.

A NEW LOVE AND NEW LIFE

In 2000, the longtime bachelor was introduced through a mutual friend to Tracie Robinson. They met backstage during a "Stars on Ice" performance and began to date immediately. He proposed to her—on the ice, of course—during a cancer benefit skating program. They were married in January of 2003. They had two children, Aidan and Maxx, and then, in 2014, they expanded their family to include Jean Paul and Evelyne, whom they adopted from Haiti.

During their courtship, Tracie's deep faith helped to reignite Scott's, which had been superficial and shallow all his life. "She took me to a minister, a man named Ken Durham. And the first thing he said to me, which was extraordinary was, he goes, 'You have to understand that Christianity is a faith of history. These things actually happened.' And I go, 'OK, that's a good starting-off point.'"[28]

When Scott was diagnosed with a benign brain tumor in 2004, it was Tracie's poise and rock-solid faith through it all that served to further solidify his own. A conversation in the middle of the night with a nurse also helped Scott appreciate the power of a personal relationship with Jesus Christ.

"Do you pray?" asked the nurse? "Yes," he replied. "What do you say when you pray?" she pressed. "I just thank God for all the blessings in my life," he responded. "Do you ask him for anything?" "No," he said. "I just want him to know I'm thankful." "Well," she said, "who is God to you?" "My father," he said quickly. "You're a father, aren't you?" she asked. "If your children needed something, wouldn't you want them to let you know?"[29]

"So, I changed the way I pray now," Scott said. "I ask. I ask uninhibitedly. For healing. For strength. For courage. I ask for another child."[30]

Scott would later point out he not only owes his skating career to his parents but also to the tumor. That's because the tumor on his pituitary gland stunted his growth. His small size, he says, is what gave him an advantage on the ice. "Who would I be without a brain tumor?" he once posited.[31]

THE BOTTOM LINE

Hamilton, who lives in Tennessee in order to be closer to Tracie's family, now runs the Scott Hamilton Skating Academy and the Scott Hamilton CARES Foundation. Tracie is heavily involved in several other philanthropic endeavors. While skating may have given Scott a life he otherwise wouldn't have had, it no longer defines him. Instead, it's his faith in the Lord by which he measures all things.

"I understand that through a strong relationship with Jesus you can endure anything," he said. "I just learned that the only true disability in life is a bad attitude. God is there to guide you through the tough spots. Every time I've gotten knocked down, I've been able to get up. Skating teaches you how to get up, because you fall down a lot. I would urge anybody to weather the storm, because on the other side of it will be something great."[32]

ADOPTION IN AMERICA

TIMELINE OF SIGNIFICANT EVENTS IN U.S. ADOPTION HISTORY[1]

1729: The first U.S. orphanage (operated by the Ursuline order of nuns) opens in Natchez, Mississippi.

1851: The "Adoption of Children Act" is passed in Massachusetts. For the first time, the focal point of the adoption process is based upon child welfare rather than adult interests.

1854: Methodist minister and philanthropist Charles Loring Brace forms the New York–based Children's Aid Society. The first "orphan trains" departs for Dowagiac, Michigan, on September 20th. All forty-six children are successfully placed in new homes.

1891: Michigan becomes the first state to require that "the [judge] shall be satisfied as to the good moral character, and the ability to support and educate such child, and of the suitableness of the home, or the person or persons adopting such child."

1898: The St. Vincent DePaul Society establishes the Catholic Home Bureau, the first Catholic agency to place children in homes rather than orphanages.

1909: President Theodore Roosevelt hosts the first White House Conference on the Care of Dependent Children. Attendees affirm the family home is "the highest and finest product of civilization."

1910–1930: The first specialized adoption agencies are founded with the intent, according to the Spence Alumni Society to "place children of unusual promise in homes of uncommon opportunities..."

1912: Congress creates the U.S. Children's Bureau in the Department of Labor "to investigate and report on all matters pertaining to the welfare of children and child life among all classes of our people."

1917: Minnesota becomes the first state to mandate "social investigation" (home studies) of all prospective adoptive families.

1919: The Russell Sage Foundation publishes the first professional child-placing manual.

1935: President Roosevelt signs into law the Social Security Act, which provides financial assistance for needy and handicapped children. This will eventually lead to the expansion of the federal government's involvement in foster care.

1937–1938: The Child Welfare League of America issues minimum standards for permanent (adoptive) and temporary (foster) placements.

1939: Valentine P. Wasson publishes *The Chosen Baby*, one of the first children's books to help parents explain adoption.

1944: Bethany Christian Home is founded by Marguerite Bonnema, Mary DeBoer, and Andrew Vandermeer on a thirteen-acre property in Grand Rapids, Michigan. They received their child placement license in 1951 and begin serving as an adoption agency.

1948: The first recorded transracial adoption of an African-American child by white parents takes place in Minnesota.

1953: Jean Paton launches Orphan Voyage, the first organization to help adoptees search for their birthparents.

1953–1958: The National Urban League Foster Care and Adoptions Project is established to help locate adoptive homes for African-American children.

1955: Bertha and Harry Holt, an evangelical couple from Oregon, are granted special permission from Congress to adopt eight Korean War orphans. Senator Richard Neuberger lauds them as examples of "the Biblical Good Samaritan." The legacy of their efforts remains today through the Holt International, an adoption agency specializing in international placements.

1970: A record 175,000 adoptions are finalized in the United States, a record number of placements for a single year.

1973: *Roe v. Wade* legalizes abortion. Over fifty-three million abortions will be performed over the course of the following four decades.

1980: Congress passes the Adoption Assistance and Child Welfare Act, legislation designed to help keep families together and, if necessary, support adoption placement if a child is removed from the home.

1981–1996: For the first time, Congress allows adoptive couples to claim a $1,500 tax deduction the year the adoption of their child was finalized. It becomes a non-refundable tax credit of $5,000 in 1997. Congress would make it permanent in 2012. By 2016, the credit was $13,460.

1997: The Adoption and Safe Families Act is passed. Experts consider it to be the most sweeping change to the nation's adoption laws in over two decades. Instead of emphasizing reunification of the biological family at all cost, legislatures agree the child's needs should come first and some children would be better off in a healthy, thriving adoptive home.

2000: Thanks to the Child Citizenship Act of 2000, foreign-born adoptees become automatic American citizens the moment they step on U.S. soil.

2015: Approximately 135,000 children are adopted in the U.S., each year, of whom 40 percent come from the foster care system. As of July 2016, 415,129 children were in the foster care system, of whom 107, 918 were available and waiting to be adopted.

CHAPTER THIRTEEN

FAITH HILL

I t's late in the summer of 1967, another sweltering season in the small, Southern town of Ridgeland, Mississippi. Like in any community, there are as many stories as there are people, and on this particular day, a fateful conversation is going on inside the home of Ted and Edna Perry.

In fact, versions of this very same discussion have been going on for months.

Thirty-seven-year-old Ted and thirty-one-year-old Edna are the proud parents of two young boys, Wesley, age eight, and Steve, age six. The family is thriving. They're healthy, happy, and deeply involved in the life of their nearby Baptist church.

Ted works at the Presto Manufacturing Company factory in neighboring Jackson. At Presto, Ted and his cohorts are responsible for helping to produce small household appliances, everything from irons to electric frying pans. Ted's no stranger to physical labor. After all, he's been employed, in some form or fashion, for nearly thirty years. One of thirteen children, he dropped out of school in the fourth grade to help support his family. As a result, he never learned to read. But he knows how to work, and he's not afraid of hard, manual labor. Prior to the arrival of their boys, Edna worked as a bank teller. She became a full-time homemaker.

Shortly after Steve arrived in 1961, Ted and Edna began praying for another child, specifically a girl, perhaps to round out the boys' rough edges and bring some young feminine gentility to the family home. And what father doesn't want a daughter, a chance to watch his wife grow up all over again? But month after month and year after year their prayers seemingly went unanswered. Perhaps it's simply not meant to be says Ted. And after all, two energetic and rambunctious boys are keeping them busy. Do they really need another child? Ted's not so sure. Edna disagrees. She senses the Holy Spirit is answering that question in the affirmative. Ted's heart is open.

Up until then they tried to grow their family through traditional means. There's no question the pain of infertility stings, but it tends to be somewhat tempered when you've already been blessed with biological children. Still, they can't get over the sense their family is not yet complete. They long to add another seat to the table.

So, how about adoption? Again, they pray. This time they both felt like it was something they should pursue. But, how are they to even go about it? It's the late 1960s and the subject of adoption is not something most people talk about in public. If it does come up in conversation, it's usually in whispers.

As August turns to September, the Perrys decide to reach out to a doctor friend. If he were to hear of a young woman looking to place her child for adoption, would he kindly let them know? As they hear themselves say it, it sounds like something of a long shot or, at least, something that could take a long time to materialize. All the pieces are going to have to fall perfectly into place. It's pretty rare for a pregnant woman to tell her doctor she's considering an adoption plan for the baby. But yes, the doctor is happy to help and promises to send out feelers.

At the time, it's almost implausible to think the Perrys would receive a call within the week, but that's exactly what's about to happen.

A PERFECT MATCH

Providentially, just a few miles away from Edna and Ted, twenty-three-year-old Paula Conway is just days away from delivery. Originally from Titusville, Florida, but temporarily living in Mississippi, she's not in a position to raise the child she's been carrying for nearly nine months. It's a heartbreaking turn of events for the young woman, but she desperately wants her baby to have what she's not currently in a position to give. It's not exactly clear why, though we do know she's not married to the baby's father, Edwin White. Paula and Edwin eventually married years later and had a son, Zachary.

So, just days after visiting with their doctor and committing their request to prayer, the Perrys received the call that would change their lives and the life of their soon-to-be adopted daughter.

A baby girl was born available for adoption. Were they interested? It was an easy decision, of course. Arrangements were made to receive her back at the doctor's office. Their son Wesley suggested they name her Audra, the name of a character in his favorite show, *Big Valley*, Audra Barkley. The Perrys modify the proposal, suggesting "Audrey" and adding the middle name of "Faith" to serve as a testimony to God's overwhelming generosity and willingness to answer prayer.

The couple is stunned but ecstatic. If only every prayer were answered so quickly and assuredly.

A MISSISSIPPI CHILDHOOD

Looking back on her birth mother's decision to make an adoption plan for her, Faith, who always knew she was adopted, recognizes the gravity of Paula's loving sacrifice. "I can't imagine the choice to do that and how thankful I am that she (Paula Conway) was able to give me the opportunity that I had because I was placed into an incredible home that I mean basically is responsible for the way I am today and the backbone that I have in order to do this for a living, which is a crazy, sometimes unstable world that this projects. But the most important thing to me is about my family and that was definitely taught from my mom and dad."[1]

Life in the Perry home was warm, loving, and stable. "I actually had a pretty amazing childhood. My family, my mom and my dad and my brothers, they are amazing," she once told Larry King. Faith's singing ability from an early age was obvious. She began singing at just three years of age, proudly parading around her family's home with a hairbrush as a microphone. Her first songs were the classic old hymns of her family's Christian faith (e.g. "Jesus Love Me") she learned within the fellowship of Star Baptist Church.

"My mom used to say that I held the hymn book upside down, pretending I could read the words," she once said.[2]

As Faith grew older, she was drawn to more secular music, specifically the legendary Elvis Presley, a fellow Mississippi native. At seven, she pleaded with her parents to take her to his concert at the Mississippi Coliseum. It was a benefit performance for victims of a local tornado. It was May 5, 1975. Her conservative mother resisted, citing concerns about the bad influence of rock and roll. A neighbor intervened and convinced Edna it would be alright. She relented.

For Faith Hill, the experience of that single night convinced her music was to be her future.

"I sat in the top row of the arena and I remember everyone going wild," she said. "But it was as if there was nobody there—except for me and Elvis."[3]

Adorned in a baby blue leisure suit and rotating blue and white scarves between numbers, "The King" duly impressed one of his youngest fans in the audience. "I'm not sure what it was," she remembered. "His presence, the reaction of the people, I don't know. But what I did know was that after that concert, I had to be a performer, pure and simple."[4]

CULTURAL TENSION

So, life was happy at home and music thrilled her soul, but Faith's childhood wasn't all sweetness and light. Perhaps the most significant challenge of her formative years involved having to navigate the lingering racial tensions in and around Jackson. When Faith was just three, a Vietnam War protest at nearby Jackson State College turned deadly. Police, responding to reports of protestors pelting white motorists with rocks, wound up killing two black students. The aftermath of the incident left scars in the community, including at Faith's school, McLaurin Attendance Center in Florence. She never got wrapped up in any of the tension, but was aware it was there. How could she not be?

As Faith matured, a mischievous streak began to emerge in her adolescence. Although music served as her primary interest (her first public performance took place at a women's luncheon when she was just ten), she often found herself in the middle of immature and even destructive high jinks with her friends. For example, just after Faith entered the fifth grade, a new housing facility was constructed up the street from the family's home. Faith and her friends found the newly installed windows too tempting to ignore and wound up breaking most of them by throwing rocks. Here's how Faith remembers the incident:

"The police were called, and my mom stopped the police before they got down there, and she said, 'You just let her have it. You do whatever you have to do to scare her to death because once she gets home, she's going to wish she'd not come home.'"[5]

"So we heard the police coming, and we ran really fast around the workmen's trailer, and we were hiding behind the trailer, and I was thinking, *My life's about to end right now, and I'm only ten years old.*"[6]

"Sure enough, the cop got us, and took us back home, and he said, 'I'm putting your name on this list. If you ever do this again, you're going to jail.'"[7]

HUMBLED AND CONVICTED

The incident rattled the future country star. She was sincerely repentant and promised her father she would cut out her antics—or at least any antics that could land her in jail. Her father wasn't permissive, but he was a lot easier going than her mom. Ted knew Edna's limits and urged Faith to behave, but also to not tell her mother everything. It would make for a happier home life.

By the time Faith turned eleven, her parents decided to find a smaller, more tranquil setting for the family of five. They found it twenty miles to the southeast of Jackson in the quaint town of Star, Mississippi. Far enough away to find that feeling of rural life, but still close enough for Ted to commute to his job at Presto and the kids to remain in school in Florence, the Perrys settled easily into their new surroundings.

Much to her parents' dismay, Faith's rebellious streak continued to reveal itself. She and her girlfriends enjoyed playing "Chicken" with the freight trains that roared through the center of town. Side by side they walked the tracks, waiting to see the headlight, listening for the piercing whistle of the engine's warning. The last girl to jump from the tracks was considered to be the "bravest"—a moniker Faith often won.

As a teenager, the singing prodigy had lots of other interests besides music. She was a member of her high school's drama club, played basketball, ran track, was the official baseball scorekeeper, served on student council, was even a cheerleader, and was eventually elected homecoming queen.

She was tall, talented, attractive, and popular, but still struggling with her self-confidence.

HIGH SCHOOL ROMANCE

Sidney Wheatley was Faith's first serious boyfriend. For the rising music star, he was straight from central casting. Handsome, popular, and the top athlete in school, serving as the lead pitcher in baseball and quarterback in football, the two became the school's inseparable power couple.

At home, however, the seriousness of the relationship concerned both Faith's and Sidney's parents. Ted and Edna were concerned Faith would end up heartbroken or an unwed mother. Sidney's parents preferred their son focus on academics and sports.

"I got in trouble for staying on the phone at night too late, getting phone calls past nine o'clock in high school," Faith once lamented. "I would always be the one to get in trouble."[8]

The two year courtship ended at the conclusion of their junior year. At the urging of his parents, Sidney broke it off. Faith was devastated.

Through it all, however, Faith Perry's church family remained the one constant and stabilizing force in her life.

"Growing up, my friends and I would hang out in the parking lot after church at Star Baptist Church, planning our lives and sharing our dreams," she remembered fondly. Being a dreamer, Faith struggled with contentment. "This [Star] is a dreadful place," she once told a friend. "I've got to find a way to get out quick. I can't wait until I'm eighteen or nineteen."[9]

SEEKING THE SPOTLIGHT

Looking for the big break that would allow her to shake the dust of Star from her shoes, Faith looked for every opportunity to perform, a habit often landing her in colorful and eccentric venues. When she was sixteen, she agreed to compete in a tobacco-spitting contest after she learned the winner was awarded time to sing in front of all the contestants and crowd. She chewed, spit—and won.

"They cleaned the stage off with towels, and then I went on," Faith recalled.[10]

Many of her friends recall her singing "Amazing Grace" and the National Anthem at school events. She clearly had a gift. "We had no doubt she would do it [sing professionally]," said Robin Byrd, a childhood friend.[11]

THAT LITTLE MYSTERY

Although Faith always knew she was adopted, the story she was told regarding her birthparents wasn't actually true. Perhaps her parents were trying to spare her of any trauma associated with the facts. There's always the chance they weren't aware of the truth either. Either way, as Faith matured, she wondered and even fantasized about her origins. Were her biological parents now rich and famous? Did they live just a few towns over? Had she ever unknowingly crossed paths with them? She was curious.

"I had been told that [my birth mother] had an affair with a married man, and he didn't want to leave his wife to marry her, so she gave me up for adoption," Faith has said. "But it was completely untrue."[12]

It should be noted, however, that Faith's parents never objected to her search for details. They didn't necessarily know things she didn't. In Mississippi, as elsewhere, adoption records are sealed by the court. And in the days before the ease of searching on the Internet, information surrounding such matters was often difficult to ascertain.

SEARCHING FOR FAME AND FAMILY

In the fall of 1986, having graduated from high school the previous spring and unsure of what to do, Faith decided to enroll in Hinds Community College. Her brothers urged her to continue her education and her mom and dad were pleased with her decision. She remained living at home and commuted each day to class. To help pay for tuition, Faith took a job on the school's recruiting team, a position well suited to her outgoing and gregarious temperament. The role also provided her an opportunity to sing in conventional venues, like at a reception for the Fellowship of Christian Athletes and sometimes in unusual places, too, like the Hinds County Jail.

"I'd go in and sing 'Amazing Grace,' and sometimes read a Bible verse or something, or give a testimony, just talk about what I was doing in school, and something that happened in my life," Faith remembered.[13] She was always well received.

Just like in high school, the nineteen-year-old also got along well with her classmates. Her supervisor, Bill Buckner, was immediately impressed. But Buckner remembers she was still unsettled about not only her future but also her past. She remained curious about her birth parents. "The people that took her in," said Bill, referring to Faith's adoptive parents, "she loved them and did not want to hurt them, but inside she had this yearning to know."[14]

That Faith would confide so quickly in people she just met spoke to the depth of her desire to finally put the pieces to the puzzle of her life together.

Uncertainty in one area of life often magnifies frustrations in another. Might her fierce curiosity regarding her biological parents propel her to finally put feet to her dreams to launch a music career? The timing would certainly suggest that was the case.

After just one semester, Faith announced she was leaving Hinds Community College to pursue her music in Nashville. Nearly everyone tried to talk her out of it. It was too much of a long shot, they insisted. "Many try but few succeed," she was told. Did she really want to risk rejection? Faith listened, but she still couldn't shake the memories of that magical night twelve years earlier at the Elvis concert inside the Mississippi Coliseum.

Could the fantasy of a seven-year-old really become reality? She was determined to find out.

NASHVILLE OR BUST

Looking back, it was an adventurous, even romantic scene unfolding outside the Perry home in March of 1987. Ironically, it had all the elements of a country song, minus the jilted lover. The day of the big move arrived. A couple of neighbors volunteered to drive Ted and Faith to Nashville, and so there they were with the pick-up truck filled with the meager possessions of an aspiring star. Prayers were said. Tears flowed. Last hugs were given.

The two neighbors and Faith sat in the cab. Ted sat in a large cardboard box in the bed of the truck. One can only imagine how Edna felt watching her only daughter drive away into the light of that early spring morning. How had nineteen years gone so quickly? She was their dream come true—and now she was about to chase hers, on her own—eight hours away. Only parents will understand the competing emotions that ran through Ted and Edna.

"They realized this was my dream," said Faith. "[My parents] just had to pray they'd given me a solid backbone, and they knew if I wanted to come home, I could."[15]

At first, things didn't go so well. "I really believed I'd just get on the Grand Ole Opry stage, start singin', and be on a bus travelin' the next day," she recalled.[16] But Faith struggled to find even a menial job to support herself. Most employers weren't thrilled at the prospect of hiring an aspiring singer who would likely quit within months, if not weeks. The rejection took its toll on her.

"I was really confused because I felt I'd really gotten myself in a bind," she said. "I didn't know how to deal with it. So I called my mom up, and I said, 'Mom, did I ever want to be anything else in my life besides a singer, like a nurse?' And she said, 'Nope. This is what you've always wanted to do.' So she said, 'You need to hang up the phone and get busy, and just not worry about other things.' So I did. And I started to see myself again as a singer."[17]

LOVE AND WORK

In the midst of searching for a job, Faith met a gentleman named Daniel Sawyer Hill, an executive with a music publishing company. The two immediately hit it off. Hill wound up helping Faith land a job as a receptionist with Gary Morris's music company. More important, Daniel helped keep her focus on her dream. Before long they were married.

"She was charming, talented, ambitious," Daniel recalled. "But she was also confused. She moved to Nashville to sing, but at times she would get frustrated with the music business, and her priorities seemed to shift toward more domestic pursuits, such as cooking and decorating our home. She even considered enrolling in interior design school. I always tried to steer her back toward music, where I knew her true talent was."[18]

Despite that talent, Faith continued to struggle. She hung out at cafes and clubs, sang whenever she was given the opportunity and often gave voice to the compositions of aspiring songwriter friends. Finally, nearly five years after arriving in Nashville, Faith received a recording contract from Warner Brothers. She was on her way.

At the same time, Faith and Daniel's marriage was falling apart. "I was going through so much. I was like a flower trying to bud," she said.

"Marriage wasn't what I needed. It was a disguise. That's not to say anything bad about the person I married. But what I needed was to deal with the issues of my own life."[19]

THE SEARCH

For Faith, that primary issue was solving the mystery of her birth mother's identity. For that, she employed the help of her brother, Wesley, who, armed with a social security number, combed through city directories of the Jackson Public Library. At last, he found Paula Conway. An intermediary was arranged to contact Paula, just in case she didn't want to meet Faith. But she did and she was eager to do so.

"The first time I met [my birth mother], I just stared at her," Faith said. "I'd never seen anyone that looked anything like me. It was the awe of seeing someone you came from. It fills something."[20]

SADNESS AND HOPE

For Faith Hill, meeting her birth mother turned out to be a watershed moment in her life. Prior to meeting her, she has said she felt "lost." That feeling was gone. Although saddened to learn her birth father was killed in a car accident ten year after her birth, the mystery was finally solved. In meeting her birth mother she also learned she had a full-brother, Zachary. It was as if a long-lost piece from a cherished puzzle was found. Kathy Jones, a childhood friend, said, "She felt like somebody had just lifted a huge weight off her life. She was able to move on."[21]

Unfortunately, by then, her marriage had already deteriorated to the point of no return. After five years together, Faith and Daniel decided to divorce. It was amicable. "I think she had a reality check," said Gary Morris, her boss at the time. "She grew up and changed her views about what was important to her."[22]

Faith arrived in Nashville an anxious, starry-eyed teenager. In Daniel she found someone not only to love and love her—but also a sense of security. In the five years since she arrived, Faith, by her own admission, matured on several levels. She satisfied her desire to meet her biological mother. She realized she married impulsively as a teenager for many of the wrong reasons. And, she landed a record deal. She released her first album, *Take Me As I Am*, in 1993. She was on her way.

REMARRIAGE AND FAMILY

Faith Hill first met fellow country singer Tim McGraw at a Nashville radio station, but they didn't start dating until performing together on tour in 1996. They married shortly thereafter. Faith and Tim quickly became one of country music's most popular and beloved couples. It's a reality that comes at a price. Paparazzi and press track their every move. Some of their relationship challenges as a couple have been played out in the tabloids, most of it exaggerated or patently false. Now together for twenty years, the first couple of Nashville remain committed to one another.

"My husband and I have made the choice that our marriage is the most important thing to us," Hill recently explained. "We respect what we have and understand how we need to feed it."[23] From their marriage they have three daughters—Gracie Katherin, Maggie Elizabeth, and Audrey Caroline.

Tim, who discovered at age eleven he was adopted by his step-father at birth, is in a place to understand and appreciate the unique road Faith has traveled. That road, however, was the route that led to Faith's stardom. From Edna's encouragement to Ted's guidance and cooperation, Faith credits her adoptive mother and father with preparing her for the life she now lives. From the ticket to see Elvis to laying a solid Christian foundation, Faith was shaped in so many ways by Ted and Edna.

Faith also gives credit to her biological mother, a woman whose sacrificial choice first set the course for her journey.

"I have a lot of respect for her," Faith said of Paula Conway, "and I had no feelings of anger or any of that...I know she must have had a lot of love for me to want to give me what she felt was a better choice. Thank God she let me live."[24]

CHAPTER FOURTEEN

JOHANN SEBASTIAN BACH

I t was an assignment almost too cruel to fathom.

Nine-year-old Johann Sebastian Bach, the youngest of eight children in his musical family, was standing outside in the bone-chilling cold of February 24th. He was alongside his fellow choir members, each wearing their chorister cassocks, which did little to protect against the frigid winter wind. Snow blanketed the ground of the old cemetery of Eisenach, Germany. The year was 1795, and the assembly was there to lay to rest the town's esteemed Kapellmeister—the forty-nine-year-old director of the town's musicians as well as the court trumpeter for the Duke of Eisenach in Thuringia.

The name of the deceased?

Johann Ambrosius Bach. Johann Sebastian's father.

Just eight months earlier the young boy stood in the same spot for the funeral of his mother, Maria Elisabeth Lammerhirt. She was just fifty years of age. Only three years earlier, Johann Sebastian attended the funeral of his brother, Balthasar, who died at eighteen. His brother

Johann Jonas and sister Johanna Juditha died two years apart, when Johann Sebastian was still an infant. Still, no one ever grows accustomed to death, especially the loss of loved ones.

As the slow procession from the church settled around the gravesite, the future composer joined in the singing of Martin Luther's hymn, *In the Very Midst of Life*. For the grief-stricken youth, the lyrics hit far too close to home:

"In the very midst of life, snares of death surround us; Who shall help us in the strife, lest the foe confound us?"[1]

That so much sorrow could befall a child at such a formative time of life was, sadly, not all that uncommon in eighteenth century Europe. Plagues, disease, and poor hygiene, along with inadequate nutrition, contributed to early mortality. In the day and age of Bach, even childhood itself was a leading cause of death. Of all the passings of his era, over one-third were children under the age of five. Even if you made it out of childhood, the average life expectancy was still under forty years of age.

But all of the statistics and averages were meaningless to the grief-stricken Johann Sebastian. It's one thing to lose one parent—but to lose two and so close together was a devastating hardship beyond comprehension. He was left an orphan in search of a home.

EARLY LIFE

In the Thuringia region of Germany, the name "Bach" was synonymous with music. In fact, it was said music was the family business. Beginning in the middle of the sixteenth century, members of the family held numerous important musical positions throughout the region, publishing and performing popular compositions of the day. Historians trace the start of the dynasty back to Johann Sebastian's great, great grandfather, Veit Bach. The elder Bach escaped Moravia or Slovakia during the Schmalkaldic War, a period of violence centered on the expulsion of Protestants in the Counter-Reformation. The patriarch Bach was actually a baker by trade, but also played the cittern, a stringed instrument similar to a lute.

From that simple lineage over two hundred years later emerged Johann Ambrosius Bach—a talented musician who arrived in the nearby town of Erfurt in 1667 to assume the role of town piper. The European tradition of such a position stemmed from the belief communities needed a rallying point from which to both make announcements and encourage its citizens. In addition to the trumpet, Johann Ambrosius also played the violin. When Christoph Schmidt, the town piper of nearby Eisenach, died in 1670, Schmidt's daughter, who was married to Johann's cousin, recommended him for the position. He was quickly hired.

Arriving in Eisenach, a town with a population of approximately six thousand people, the role of town piper came with two primary responsibilities. Johann Ambrosius's first task was to perform each day at the town hall with five other musicians at ten o'clock in the morning and five o'clock in the evening. They would play Abblassen—a triumphant trumpet fanfare. He was also expected to lead worship services at St. George's Church, a parish first established in the twelfth century and with a pulpit from which Martin Luther preached in 1521. In addition to planning and performing music for all Sunday services, Johann Ambrosius was also responsible for the music of feast days and afternoon vespers. He was a man in his element from the moment he arrived.

The popular musician was also in high demand for playing in a variety of other venues, including weddings and dinner parties. From these extracurricular events he made as much income as from his full-time assignment. As a result, the Bachs lived comfortably, though not ostentatiously. Given his role in the town's music circles, the family regularly hosted apprentice musicians, who lived alongside other Bachs in the house. Ambrosius enjoyed his role as teacher and mentor.

RISING REPUTATION

By the time Johann Sebastian arrived on March 21, 1685, his father's musical gifts were being widely lauded. "His particular professional qualifications," one reviewer wrote, "in that he can come up with vocal and instrumental music for worship service and for honorable assemblies with persons of higher and lower ranks in such a way that we cannot remember having ever experienced anything like it in this place."[2] Yet another stated, "The new town piper made music with organ, violins, voices, trumpets, and military drums as had never before been done by any cantor or town musician as long as Eisenach stood."[3]

Surrounded by music and musicians, Sebastian took to the family business at an early age. His father taught him how to play both the violin and the harpsichord. He also spent considerable time with his uncle, Johann Christoph, the renowned organist at St. George's in Eisenach. Christoph schooled him in the finer points of the keyboard. Sebastian later refered to him as not just an accomplished player but also a "profound composer" who was "strong in the invention of beautiful ideas as well as in the expression of the meaning of the words." His writing, he said, was "gallant" and his singing was "remarkably polyphonous."[4]

When it came to Ambrosius's musical tasks and functions, all the Bach children were pressed into service in some form or fashion. As a child, Sebastian helped clean brass, restring fiddles, carry instruments, turn pages for musicians, and help set up and tear down from performances. Before Sebastian turned eight he was proficient with all three of the instruments in his care—the violin, harpsichord, and keyboard. More importantly, he loved music and everything about it.

A DIFFICULT HOME LIFE

Given the family pedigree, it would be easy to assume Sebastian's early childhood was charmed, a seemingly endless series of fortunate and talented connections, each one steadily marching the boy toward his eventual greatness.

It was, in fact, anything but a life of ease.

While enjoying the stability and benefits of married and committed parents, the deaths of his older siblings cast a long and sorrowful shadow on the Bach home. Johann Ambrosius and Maria Elisabeth, of course, took both deaths extremely hard. After all, you can't ever replace a child.

As the saying goes, sometimes "the smallest things take up the most room in your heart."[5] For the Bachs, the loss of their children left them physically and emotionally bereft. Yet, they had no choice but to carry on given their professional responsibilities, the remaining children in their care, and the pressing needs still present in their house.

Some of those needs involved caring for Dorothea Maria, Ambrosius's mentally and physically handicapped younger sister. Elisabeth's widowed mother, Eva Barbara Lammerhirt, also lived with the family. She moved in to help with the growing clan given the increasingly busy schedule of the town piper. As time went on, they began caring for her.

Through it all, Sebastian was watching and absorbing. A deeply introspective youngster, he was internalizing the pain, sorrow, and frustration he was witnessing and feeling first hand. In time, he began to channel it all into his musical compositions. A deeply religious boy, Sebastian was well-versed in the Scriptures, even as a young boy. In them he found solace and comfort from the arrows of life, believing ultimately, God was sovereign over all things. He could think of no other way to process the pain than to trust in his Creator and believe the angst would one day be redeemed. Speaking of the timeless pain of grief, he would later say, "God's gift to his sorrowing creatures is a joy worthy of their destiny."[6]

ACADEMIC RIGORS

All of the Bach children attended the famous St. George's Latin school in Eisenach, the same institution where Martin Luther once attended back at the turn of the sixteenth century. At St. George's, religious instruction was intertwined with all the arts and sciences. To be sure, faith and science were not only compatible but inseparable. "Why do you go to school?" the children were regularly asked. To which they would respond, "So that I may grow up righteous and learned."[7] Arriving in 1692, Sebastian's required reading included Luther's Catechism and the Old Testament Psalms. Daily instruction in writing, reading, and grammar—both in German and in Latin—was the norm.

Although the records indicate Sebastian missed forty-eight days of school in 1693, twenty-nine in 1694, and fifty-one in 1695—likely due to illness and the deaths of his parents—he nevertheless excelled academically. In 1694, he was ranked fourteenth out of seventy-four students. One of his favorite pastimes, however, was singing in the school's St. Georgenkirche choir, a privilege his idol and inspiration Martin Luther had also done as a young boy. According to one account, the boy who would become the world's most famous composer had "an uncommonly fine treble voice."[8]

For the rising adolescent there was great symmetry and inspiration in the historical arc of Christian life in Eisenach. From his perch in the choir loft he could see the font where both he and Martin Luther were baptized, albeit two hundred years apart. He knew the sacred words spoken and sung within the walls of the sanctuary were not only the same words generations before had heard—but the wisdom contained within the words and music was timeless and true.

In the years to come he would be forced to lean even more heavily on those foundational truths.

TRAGEDY

We know Sebastian's mother, Elisabeth, died on May 1, 1694. Was she ill or was the death sudden? Sadly, all that is known of her passing is from a single entry in the death registry of St. George's Church. It doesn't even contain her name. The entry reads as follows:

May 3, 1694. Buried, Johann Ambrosius Bach's wife–without fee.[9]

Ambrosius, now a widower with young children, was deeply shaken. What was he to do? Shortly after the death he reached out to Barbara Margharetha, a twice-widowed friend from Arnstadt who was once married to a musician and instrument-builder friend. She had two daughters, aged twelve and ten. Ambrosius and Barbara began courting and were married in the Bach home on November 27, 1694.

Unfortunately, shortly thereafter, Ambrosius fell seriously ill. As his widow recorded, the famed town piper died just "twelve weeks and one day" from the date of their wedding.[10]

So in less than ten months, Sebastian lost both a mother and a father—and within thirteen years, Barbara lost three husbands. After helping to ensure the musical needs of the community were met, she decided to take her daughters and return to live with family in Arnstadt. Ambrosius's two sons, Jacob and Sebastian, would be entrusted to the care of their older brother, Johann Christoph.

ADOPTED IN OHRDRUF

At twenty-four years of age, Johann Christoph had only recently been installed as the organist at St. Michael's in Ohrdruf. The oldest son in the Bach family, Johann Christoph was still a newlywed. He married Johanna Dorothea Vonhoff, the daughter of the Ohrdruf's town councillor just months earlier on October 23, 1694.

Accepting the responsibility of raising and nurturing a newly minted ten-year-old and a thirteen-year-old was no small task for Christoph and Johanna Dorothea, but they quickly assimilated as a newly formed family of four. Christoph enrolled the boys in the local Lutheran Latin school, Ohrdruf Lyceum Illustre. The instruction was as rigorous and demanding as it was back in Eisenach, and Sebastian thrived, rising to the top of his class in 1697.

THE POWER OF INFLUENCE

Although still young, Christoph was already a highly accomplished musician. He studied for three years under Johann Pachelbel, a man many considered to be the dominant figure in seventeenth-century organ music. Pachelbel composed both sacred and secular pieces, including what is considered to be his master work, *Hexachordum Apollinis*, a work which contains six Arias with six variations in six different keys for the harpsichord or organ.

There's no record of Sebastian having met Pachelbel, but Christoph worked tirelessly to relay to his younger brother what the master taught him. The instruction came at just the right time, too. The young Sebastian was eager to put into practice what he saw and heard all his life. Christoph began instructing the youngster in the art of the clavichord, a stringed keyboard musical instrument. Usually rectangular in shape, the clavichord was popular between 1400 and 1800.

In addition, thanks to Pachelbel's training, Christoph introduced Sebastian to many of the leading composers of the day. These included north German artists Johann Jakob Froberger and French musicians Jean-Baptiste Lully and Marin Marais. Their respective and collective works filled the young Bach with a spirit of awe and wonder. If they could compose such music, well then surely he could also.

There were times when this dream and drive compelled Sebastian to go to great lengths in order to accomplish it.

On a lattice-locked bookshelf in Christoph and Dorothea's home stood a book containing the compositions of Bach's newest heroes. Since the book was fragile and valuable, Christoph forbade the adolescent from handling it. Determined and defiant, he snuck out of his bedroom each night and, using his small hand, pulled the rolled up book through the lattice. Then, since he was prohibited from lighting candles, he copied each piece of music by moonlight. It took him six months to finish the task.

ORGAN FAILURES

Originally settled by Scottish-Irish missionary monks in 727, the small but influential parish of Ohrdruf, twenty-five miles southeast of Eisenach, had two organs on the property. In addition to the one inside the church there was also one in the hospital chapel, both of which Christoph was responsible to play and maintain. The larger instrument in the church was relatively new, having only been installed in 1675. Unfortunately, though, the installation was incomplete. As a result, the organ never really worked properly. It was determined pieces were missing or in need of repair, but the instrument's maker, Heinrich Brunner of Sandersleben, delayed work for years. It became such a controversy and frustration even the town council threatened to seize Brunner's assets. In all, it would take nearly fifteen years to properly fix the instrument.

It was the future British Prime Minister Benjamin Disraeli who once observed "There is no education like adversity," and for the young Sebastian, such was the case when it came to the organ woes of his home parish.[11] Through it all, the youngster had a front row seat. He learned first-hand not only how an organ worked—but how to fix it if it broke. This real-life experience proved invaluable to him in his future work as both a composer and organist.

MAKING HIS MUSIC HIS OWN

By 1700 Sebastian was fifteen years old and Christoph wanted him to experience what he had at his age—an opportunity to leave home and study under some of the leading lights of the day. Though most in his circle preferred he stay within the region, Sebastian chose to break with family tradition (no Bach had ever ventured out of the area). He accepted a scholarship to study choral music at St. Michael's School in Luneberg, an institution two hundred and thirty-eight miles to the north of Ohrdruf. In order to pay for his room and board, Sebastian sang in the choir.

Though sad to see him go, Christoph and Dorothea wholeheartedly supported his decision. He was yearning for his independence and establishing his own identity. In 1704, Sebastian's older brother Jacob also left home to join the military band for the army of King Charles XII of Sweden.

UNIQUELY PREPARED FOR THE FUTURE

Arriving in Luneberg, a person would have been hard-pressed to find a student more prepared for a life of success than Johann Sebastian Bach. His bona fides were unsurpassed. Academically, he was at the top of his class. Musically, he had been exposed to the very best talent and teachers in all of Europe.

After graduating from St. Michael's in 1703, Sebastian followed in the footsteps of his father and family and went on to hold a variety of professional music positions throughout Germany, including roles as a Kapellmeister, cantor, violinist, and numerous jobs as head church organist. His robust playing often surprised congregations accustomed to more sedate music. One church even threatened to reprimand him for his unorthodox style, but later relented, citing his youth.

LEGENDARY COMPOSER

It would be in the midst of his daily responsibilities that Sebastian composed some of his most famous and lasting pieces, including St. Matthew Passion, St. John Passion, and the Christmas Oratorio. He was singularly prolific. His creativity seemed to increase the tighter the deadline and the greater the demands on his time. While serving as a church organist, Sebastian wrote a cantata *every week*—more than three hundred in total.

FAMILY MAN

In 1706, twenty-one-year-old Sebastian married Maria Barbara Bach, a second cousin. They had seven children, only four of whom made it out of childhood. After Maria died in 1720, Bach remarried a year later to Anna Magdalena Wulcken, a singer. In addition to raising the children from Sebastian's first marriage, the couple had thirteen of their own, only six of whom lived into adulthood.

THE KEY TO HIS GREATNESS

At a time when he was most vulnerable—losing both a mother and father at just nine years of age—Johann Sebastian Bach's immediate needs weren't just met—he was loved and nurtured and told he mattered.

Simply put, Christoph and Dorothea's decision in 1695 to adopt him as one of their own didn't just change the trajectory of Sebastian's life, it changed the course of music and the faith, and very possibly even the eternity of countless individuals in the world. How so?

"THE FIFTH EVANGELIST"

"The main purpose of my music is to glorify God," Sebastian once wrote. "Some people do this with music that is simple. I haven't chosen to use a simple style. But my music comes from my heart as a humble offering to God. This honors God no matter what musical style I use."[12]

With his ability to compose music that engages both the mind and the heart, Johann Sebastian Bach, more than two centuries after his death, has gained a reputation for leading people to Christ through his music. Yet when peers and contemporaries would attempt to laud him, he was always quick to give the Lord the credit.

"I play the notes as they are written," he once famously said. "But it is God who makes the music...The aim and final end of all music should be none other than the glory of God and the recreation of the soul."[13]

Indeed, when composing his music, Bach would write "JJ" across the top of his sheet music ("Jesus help me") and would sign every manuscript "SDG" (Soli Deo Gloria—Only for the glory of God).

"The music of my father," wrote his son Carl Phillip Emmanuel Bach, "[had] higher intentions. It's not supposed to fill the ear but to make your heart move."[14]

A FINAL PIECE

Appropriately, Johann Sebastian Bach composed his last work, "The Art of the Fugue," on his deathbed in 1750. The piece contained a succession of notes based on the letters in his name – B – A – C – H*. Blind and feeble, the ailing composer was forced to dictate his words, which he did, and offered one last chorale to his son-in-law. The words would serve to be his final ones on earth: *Vor deinen Thron tret' ich hier-mit* (Before thy throne I come herewith).

A moment later, he was dead.

CHAPTER FIFTEEN

LEO TOLSTOY

When the Russian writer Count Lev Nikolayevich, otherwise known as Leo Tolstoy, published his first novel in 1852, the story was purported to be a work of fiction, which was technically true. Titled *Childhood* and released in the Russian literary journal, *The Contemporary*, the narrative is written from the point of view of an adult named Nikolenka who is looking back on life as a ten-year-old boy.

"Will that freshness, that happy carelessness, that necessity for love and strength of faith, which you possessed in childhood, ever return?" the character Nikolenka ponders.[1] "Can anytime be better than that when the true greatest virtues—innocent gayety and unbounded thirst for love—were the only requirements of life?"[2]

For Nikolenka—and Tolstoy personally—the questions were largely rhetorical. In time, *Childhood*, and the subsequent books in the trilogy series, *Boyhood* and *Youth*, were seen to be autobiographical. Written and released when he was just twenty-three years of age, the storyline contrasts such wistfulness and nostalgia about the joys of the carefree days as a child with the hard realities of love and loss in life.

"Mama was dead, but our life pursued its usual course," Nikolenka laments later in the book, describing the sad scene of his mother's passing. "Went to bed and got up at the same hours, and in the same rooms; morning and evening tea, dinner, supper, all took place at the usual time; the tables and chairs stood in the same places; nothing was changed in the house or in our manner of life, only—she was no more."[3]

The grieving Nikolenka continues to struggle with what he considers to be cruel indifference to his loss. "It seemed to me that, after such a catastrophe, all must change; our ordinary manner of life appeared to me an insult to her memory, and recalled her absence too vividly."[4]

For Leo Tolstoy, Nikolenka Irten'ev's character was deeply personal, a reflection of some of the deepest pain and sorrow of his own childhood—anguish still very real and fresh.

FAMILY ROOTS

Leo Tolstoy was born on August 28, 1828, the fourth child of a wealthy, aristocratic family in Russia's Tula province. His father, Count Nikolai Ilyich Tolstoy, once served in the army and was captured by Napoleon's invading forces in 1812. When the young soldier was released two years later, Nikolai discovered that in his absence, his family suffered a major financial reversal—his father gambled their money away. The prospect of a comfortable inheritance and lifestyle gone, Nikolai received an appointment in Russia's military bureaucracy and began toiling away on honest but unremarkable work.

As so often occurred, a poor man who wanted to be rich had only two realistic options in those days—accept his circumstances or marry into money. In Leo's future mother, Maria Nikolayevna Volkonskaya, Nikolai found his golden ticket. Maria was the youngest daughter of Nikolay Sergeyevich Volkonsky, a one-time Russian ambassador to

Berlin and commander-in-chief who served Catherine the Great. In 1784, Volkonskaya inherited Yasnaya Polyana, a sprawling four-thousand-acre country estate located seven-and-a-half miles from Tula, Russia. The family poured considerable money and effort into expanding the property, which contained hundreds of serfs.

WORKING CLASS SYMPATHIES

When speaking of his grandfather, Tolstoy stressed the fairness with which he managed the help on the estate. "He was regarded as a very exacting master, but I never heard instances of his cruelty or of his inflicting the severe punishments which were usual at that time," he said. "I believe that such cases did occur on his estate, but that the enthusiastic respect for his character and intelligence was so great among the servants and the peasants of his time, whom I have often questioned about him, that although I have heard condemnation of my father, I heard only praises of my grandfather's intelligence, business capacities, and interest in the welfare of the peasants and of his enormous household. He erected splendid accommodation for his servants, and took care that they should always be not only well fed, but also well dressed and happy. On fete days he arranged recreations for them, swings, dancing, etc."[5]

Over the course of his life, Tolstoy famously championed the dignity and rights of the working and peasant classes. However, according to the Russian revolutionary G. V. Plekhanov, "The suffering of the peasants interested Tolstoy far less than those who made them suffer—the people of his own class—the landowners."[6]

Looking back on his grandfather's life and habits, Tolstoy stressed the multiplying benefits of treating people well. "Like every intelligent landowner of that time, he was concerned with the welfare of the peasants, and they prospered, the more so that my grandfather's high position, inspiring respect as it did in the police and local authorities, exempted them from oppression from this quarter."[7]

EARLIEST MEMORIES

From his autobiography we learn Leo Tolstoy's earliest memory, remarkably, is being uncomfortably swaddled in blankets. "I am bound; I wish to free my arms and I cannot do it and I scream and cry, and my cries are unpleasant to myself, but I cannot cease," he writes. "Somebody bends down over me, I do not remember who. All is in a half light. But I remember that there are two people. My cries affect them; they are disturbed by my cries, but do not unbind me as I desire, and I cry yet louder."[8]

Tolstoy acknowledges the implausibility of such a vivid memory at such a young age and allows it might have been a dream. "But certain it is that this was my first and most powerful impression in life," he wrote. "Nor is it my cries that are impressed upon my mind, nor my sufferings, but the complexity and contrast of the impression. I desire freedom, it interferes with no one else, and I, who require strength, am weak, whilst they are strong."[9]

TRAGEDY

Although he has no memory of it, Tolstoy's mother, Maria Niko-layevna, died in 1830, shortly after the birth of the couple's fifth child, Maria. She was forty years of age. His mother and father's marriage appears to have been somewhat strained. His father, Nikolai, was often away on business, once prompting Maria to write him a note, pleading him to not forget her or the children. "My sweet friend," came the reply, "you finish your last letter by asking me not to forget you; you are going mad: can I forget that which constitutes the most noble part of myself?"[10]

No picture of Maria has ever been found, a fact that never seemed to bother her youngest son. "All that I know about her is beautiful," he wrote. "And I think this has come about not merely because all who spoke to me of my mother tried to say only what was good but because there actually was much good in her."[11]

AUNT TOINETTE

Then a widower with five children, Nikolai quickly made arrangements to find assistance in helping to raise the children. Tatyana Ergol-
sky, a distant cousin already living at Yasnaya Polyana, was asked to step
in as caretaker. She enthusiastically agreed to lend a hand. Tatyana had,
herself, been an orphan who was adopted and raised by her grandpar-
ents, so she had a special empathy for the five children now in her charge.

According to Tolstoy, his father wanted to marry Tatyana years
earlier. "She probably loved my father and my father loved her," Tolstoy
would later write. "But she did not marry him in youth, in order that he
might marry my rich mother, and later she did not marry him because
she did not wish to spoil her pure poetic relations with him and us."[12]

In the years to come, Tatyana regreted her decision to decline Nikolai's proposal.

The children called her "Aunty" and at least externally, life continued at Yasnaya Polyana without much of a hitch. "When I remember her
she was more than forty, and I never thought about her being pretty or
not pretty," Tolstoy remembered. "I simply loved her—loved her eyes,
her smile, and her dusky, broad little hand with its energetic little cross
vein."[13] He saw her to be more than a kind woman, though she was
certainly not less than that. Leo went on to suggest she was "So resolute
and self-sacrificing...in everything."[14]

To be sure, in addition to enjoying the loving care of "Aunty," the
Tolstoy children were never physically lonely. They had one another, of
course, but other relatives also lived at the estate, including the children's
babushka—their grandmother, Pelageya Nikolayevna—who was the
mother of Tolstoy's father. As a youngster, Leo and the children thor-
oughly enjoyed her company, and she likewise enjoyed them.

One of the children's favorite memories of life with their grandmother
involved a gentleman named Lev Stepanych, a blind storyteller, who was
purchased for the family matriarch by her late husband. In the evenings,
Leo and his siblings gathered in the candlelight to hear Lev recite captivating and enchanting tales, including stories from Scheherazade's, *The One*

Thousand and One Nights. It's likely those magical evenings planted seeds in the future novelist's mind and heart concerning the power of good storytelling.

By now, Nikolai owned 793 male and 800 female serfs, over two hundred of whom were caring for the needs at Yasnaya Polyana, including baking, cooking, mending, landscaping, shoemaking—and storytelling. The rest of Nikolai's charges were deployed at the family's other properties throughout the region. This many servants made almost anything and everything possible for the Tolstoy children. As such, they enjoyed all types of outdoor fun, from horseback riding to tobogganing and swimming.

A FATHER'S INFLUENCE

Though deeply devoted to his work and business dealings, and still spending too much time on them for his family's tastes, it was clear Count Tolstoy deeply loved his children. In turn, they adored him, especially Leo, who admired his father's strong character and measured temperament. At a time when individuals often bribed government officials for favor and access, Leo never saw his father engage in such negotiation. "My father never humbled himself before any one, nor altered his brisk, merry, and often chaffing tone," wrote Tolstoy in his autobiography. "This feeling of self-respect, which I witnessed in him, increased my love and admiration for him."[15]

By all accounts, the elder Tolstoy was a gentleman who, like his father before him, treated his servants with kindness and respect. He was good humored, reluctant to use corporal punishment and found joy and wonder in nature, often going on long hikes with the children. To put it simply, Leo just loved being around his father.

THE MOSCOW MOVE

Aristocratic families in Russia didn't attend traditional schools, but were served by tutors and governesses, usually from France and Germany. At times, this was purely a practical matter. Wealthy families often lived far out in the country, which made daily transportation challenging if not altogether impossible. Such was the case with the Tolstoy children. As the children began to age, however, the older children began to find their education lacking. It was decided the family would move to a large apartment in Moscow, which would allow Leo's older brothers to receive formal academic training.

The family departed the family estate of Yasnaya Polyana in January of 1837. Considering the children, relatives, and the thirty servants they took along with them, the two-day trip was no easy excursion, especially given the snow and ice. The caravan consisted of seven carriages and a closed sleigh for Grandma Nikolayevna. Arriving in Moscow, an excited eight-year-old Leo and his family quickly settled into their new metropolitan environment.

SUDDEN DEATH

In early June, Count Tolstoy was called back to Tula on urgent business to address some problems concerning his recent purchase of another estate. Shortly after arriving, however, Leo's father suffered a massive lung hemorrhage and stroke. Within a few hours, he was dead. Rumors, which were never proven, began to spread that he was poisoned by one of his servants.

When the news reached Moscow, the family was shocked and devastated. Leo was heartbroken. He was now officially an orphan. The Count's mother reportedly cried for days. "She wept perpetually," Tolstoy would later write of his grandmother. "She died at the end of nine months from a broken heart and grief."[16]

Reeling from the loss of her almost-husband, Aunt Toinette took pen to paper and made the following journal entry. Her grief was palpable.

"A terrible day for me...I have lost what was most dear to me in all the world, the only being who loved me, who always treated me with the most affectionate and sincere consideration and who has taken all my happiness away with him. The only thing that binds me to life is that now I shall live for his children."[17]

Because he never actually saw his father die, or saw his body follow-ing his collapse, Leo struggled to believe his father and hero was really dead. In fact, walking around the streets of Moscow, he kept expecting to see his father turn a corner and introduce himself.

CHANGES AND ADOPTION

Aunt Toinette's devastation was surely exacerbated when she learned that Alexandra Osten-Saken, Nikolai's sister and closest relative would become the children's legal guardian. If only she had accepted Nikolai's marriage proposal just a year earlier, she would be the adoptive mother. But she didn't—and the legal proceedings moved forwarded unabated. The adoption, by court decree, left Alexandra, known as Aunt Aline, with the daunting responsibilities of, besides being responsible for the children's welfare, managing all the finances of the family's various estates.

It didn't take long for Aunt Aline to realize the Tolstoy family was carrying significant debt. Nikolai was something of a shrewd operator and managed to maintain the family's high-flying living with some cre-ative accounting practices. Changes had to be made. The budget needed to be cut. Serfs and servants were released. The family moved to a smaller house in Moscow. Aunt Aline also made the decision to split the family up. She remained in Moscow with sons Nicholas (age fifteen) and Sergey (age twelve), so as to allow them to continue their education. Dmitry (eleven), Leo (ten), and Marya (eight) would return to Yasnaya Polyana.

The elevation of Aunt Aline to mother/lead guardian was actually very well received by the children. Leo found her to be loving, sincere, and authentic. In fact, it would be the authenticity and strength of her Christian faith that would one day help lead him to an understanding and commitment to Jesus Christ as Leo Tolstoy's Lord and Savior.

"My aunt was a truly religious woman," he wrote upon reflection. "Her favorite occupation was reading the lives of the saints, conversing with pilgrims, crazy devotees, monks, and nuns, of whom some always lived in our house, while others only visited my aunt."[18]

A HORRIFIC BACKSTORY

That Alexandra Osten-Saken was even in a position to receive the Tolstoy children was something of a miracle. Years earlier she married Count Osten-Saken of the Baltic Provinces. The marriage quickly deteriorated when her husband, convinced they were being followed, shot her at point blank range and then proceeded to try and cut her tongue out with a razor blade. The mentally ill count was institutionalized.

Months later, however, Alexandra suffered a still-birth. The family, fearing she wouldn't be able to handle the truth after such calamity and terror, wound up taking a newborn baby from one of the many servants and told Alexandra the daughter was her own. She was named Pashenka. Tolstoy never found out when Pashenka was told the truth.

A FORMATIVE FAITH

It's likely it was Aunt Aline's tragic exposure to such sadness that helped to further solidify her faith. Biographers have taken to calling Aunt Aline "pious" because of her religious devotion, which would be accurate. But in essence, she simply lived out her faith—and practiced what she preached.

"Aunt [Aline] was not only outwardly religious, keeping the fasts, praying much, and associating with people of saintly life," Tolstoy said. "But she herself lived a truly Christian life, endeavoring not only to avoid all luxury and acceptance of service, but also, as much as possible, to serve others. She never had any money, because she gave away all she had to those who asked."[19]

MORE LOSS

On August 28, 1841—Leo Tolstoy's thirteenth birthday—his Aunt Aline moved to the Optina Pustyn Monastery to help nurse a prolonged illness, where she finally succumbed and died. Now having twice lost a mother, the death forced the family to once again face some significant changes. Guardianship of the children fell to Aunt Aline's younger sister, Pelageya, known in the family as Polina.

Polina and her husband, Vladimir Ivanovich, were living in Kazan, a city over six hundred miles west of Tula. Though the children very much wanted to remain with their Aunt Toinette, Polina refused. Her reasons were personal. Her husband, Vladimir, had once (or perhaps still did) had a romantic interest in Toinette. By the end of 1841, the Tolstoy children were relocated to Kazan.

THE END OF THE BEGINNING

For the now thirteen-year-old Leo Tolstoy, the arrival in Kazan marked the end of childhood and the beginning of a rebellious and wayward season of life. The introduction of "wine, women, and song" in his teenage years hastened his challenges, to be sure. Instead of reading the Bible, he began reading philosophy. When he attempted law school in 1844, he was described by teachers as someone "both unable and unwilling to learn." He soon dropped out.

In 1847, he inherited his beloved Yasnaya Polyana and invited his Aunt Toinette to join him and help manage the estate. Still trying to figure out what he was going to do with the rest of life, he slipped off to Moscow where he racked up huge gambling losses. In 1851, Leo, bordering on despondency and disgusted with himself for wasting time and incurring massive debt, decided, along with his brother Nicholas, to join the army. He served until the end of the Crimean War in 1855.

AUTHOR

It was during lulls in his military service that Tolstoy began writing. His aforementioned works, *Childhood* and *Boyhood*, were actually written in the midst of the war. *The Sevastopol Tales, Ruminations on War from the Perspective of a Soldier*, was also written and published prior to his release from the service.

Once back at Yasnaya Polyana, Tolstoy settled into life as a full-time writer. His name in literary circles was well-known and growing in popularity. Within a week in September of 1862, he met, fell in love with, and married seventeen-year-old Sofya Andreyevena Bers. The quick courtship was expedited by advice he received long ago from his Aunt Toinette.

"Nothing so forms a young man," she told him, "as an intimacy with a woman of good breeding."[20] Leo and Sofya went on to have thirteen children, ten of whom survived infancy. The volatile marriage lasted forty-eight years. Tolstoy began working on *War and Peace* shortly after they married. Its six volumes were published between 1863 and 1869.

SPIRITUAL CONVERSION

When Tolstoy sat down to begin writing his future classic, *Anna Karenina*, the first line of the novel summed up both his mood and the philosophical struggles of his life. "Happy families are all alike," he wrote, "every unhappy family is unhappy in its own way."[21] By 1873, the now famous and successful author was questioning everything from his success, choice of career and his accumulation of money to the purpose of life itself. By 1878 he had grown suicidal. Something had to give.

His decision to write *A Confession* in 1879 was a very deliberate attempt to come to a final peace. Tolstoy's writing was always a form of self-therapy, but never more so than now. He would later qualify his writing of *A Confession* as the "last period of my awakening to the truth which has given me the highest well-being in life and joyous peace in view of approaching death."[22]

By the time he was done with the manuscript, Tolstoy had found the hope he lost and was desperately looking to find. "Salvation does not lie in the rituals and profession of faith," he concluded, "but in a lucid understanding of the meaning of one's life."[23] For Tolstoy, the meaning of life was found in the love and salvation of Jesus Christ.

His religious awakening caused him to question some of the practices of the Russian Orthodox Church, suggesting they were corrupt on various levels. His boldness led to church officials excommunicating him, a decision that didn't seem to faze him.

In 1893, Tolstoy published *The Kingdom of God Is Within You*, a work many considered to be a capstone to his long and storied literary career. Titled after Luke's Gospel, Tolstoy makes an impassioned plea for peace and non-violence. Frustrated with entrenched philosophies that "Might makes right," the Russian wrote in his clear and forthright prose. "The most difficult subjects can be explained to the most slow-witted man if he has not formed any idea of them already," he observed. "But the simplest thing cannot be made clear to the most intelligent man if he is firmly persuaded that he knows already, without a shadow of doubt, what is laid before him."[24]

LASTING IMPACT

Literary critics are in near universal agreement that Leo Tolstoy was among the greatest novelists and literary craftsmen the world has ever seen. But was he great because of the poetic nature of his prose, the charm of his storytelling, or was it because of the power of the ideas he communicated? It's likely it was a combination of all three.

Clearly, Leo Tolstoy was a man who met his moment. In his difficult circumstances he found his calling and voice. Writers always write best when they're writing about what they know. Tolstoy's work, like his life, reflected both joy and pain. He put down on paper what so many people felt in their hearts. His stories spoke to the fears and frustrations and the hopes and dreams of ordinary men and women. Tolstoy's characters, like him, were deep and complex, individuals who so desperately wanted to understand and be understood.

Since the 1850s, his words and ideas have influenced countless millions, including Mahatma Gandhi and Dr. Martin Luther King Jr., both of whom were deeply moved by his call for non-violent protest. They attempted to put Tolstoy's words into practice—and in turn, their followers followed him. His work also inspired other popular writers, including his fellow Russian, Fydor Dostoevsky. The idea for his runaway bestselling novel, *Brothers Karamazov*, was hatched after Dostoevsky read *War and Peace*.

SPIRITUAL LEGACY

If not for Aunts Aline and Toinette, it's likely the name Leo Tolstoy would be unknown today to most outside his village or surrounding area. In fact, it would be impossible to overestimate the impact that both women had on the novelist's life. He had the raw talent, but it was his stepmothers who helped get it out.

But if Toinette helped to meet his most basic physical needs, which she did, it was Aline who fed his soul and planted the seeds of his future Christian faith and witness. At a time when he was emotionally and spiritually vulnerable, she became his rock and introduced him to the ultimate rock, Jesus Christ. Although he didn't come to true faith until later in life, he was watching and listening to Aline. She never said one thing and did the other. It would be against her faith he would later measure his own.

When Leo Tolstoy was laid to rest on the grounds of his ancestral home in November of 1910 at the age of eighty-two, two local peasants followed the procession with a painted sign that read:

> Lev Nikolayevich! The Memory of Your Goodness Will Not Die Amongst the Orphaned Peasants of Yasnaya Polyana.[25]

And so it was in the end as it was in beginning—the orphan had come home.

EMBRYO ADOPTION

B y January of 1997, John and Marlene Strege of Fallbrook, California, were growing weary of their quest to start a family. While many couples in their circumstances choose the fertility treatment known as in vitro fertilization (IVF) to help them achieve pregnancy, the couple had another related, albeit unconventional idea.

Instead of attempting to create additional embryos through the IVF process, what if they were to "adopt" one or more of the hundreds of thousands of "extra" frozen ones remaining from a woman's IVF procedure? It was a creative and intriguing idea. The Streges sought the counsel of three pastors and Dr. James Dobson, the well-known Christian psychologist and then host of the Focus on the Family radio program. Was the idea ethical? All the pastors and Dr. Dobson were in agreement. Not only was it ethical—but they both strongly encouraged it.

In response, John and Marlene began working with Ron Stoddart, a long-time family friend, who also happened to be an adoption attorney and executive director of Nightlight® Christian Adoptions in Orange

County, California. Together they formed the world's first embryo-adoption program. "We did not just want to pick an embryo off a clinic's list," Marlene recalled. "We wanted to have a formal adoption process just like any other parents would have when adopting a child."[1]

Following the completion of a traditional home study, the Streges were matched with a family. Four embryos were implanted, of which one survived. On December 31, 1998, Hannah was born. In the nearly twenty years since her arrival, Hannah and her parents have emerged as the leading champions of embryo adoption. Their advocacy has taken them all across the country, including several special invitations to the White House where they pleaded with the president and lawmakers to protect pre-born life.

HOW IT WORKS

Families may donate their embryos for reproduction anonymously through the fertility clinic that assisted them in the creation of their embryos. Or, they may actually select a family who receives their embryo(s) through an embryo adoption program. The very first adoption agency to recognize the need for helping families with remaining embryos was the aforementioned Nightlight® Christian Adoptions. Nightlight determined to apply adoption best practices learned from years of experience (international, domestic, and foster adoption) to the placement of embryos into families who would attempt to give birth to them.

The program was named Snowflakes because each embryo is a unique human being, frozen in time, a gift from God.

Using Nighlight Agency, families who choose to place their embryos through an embryo adoption program are able to select the family with whom they place their embryos. The family will provide the adopter with their medical history. The embryology report for their embryos will be given to the adopting parent's fertility clinic.

The embryo-adopting family completes a required adoption home study. The home study will help prepare the family for parenting any resulting children and communicating with the placing family. In most instances, the placing and adopting families will have full-genetic sibling children. The home study includes a background check on the adopting family members. It is a tool that also brings peace of mind to the placing family; adopting families have been properly vetted and prepared for parenting the children who join their family in this unique way.

The agency then works with both the placing and adopting families to help them mutually agree upon the placement and to outline their plans for future communications. The embryo adoption model encourages an open placement for the benefit of all: placing parents, adopting parents, and all genetic siblings.

The legal side of embryo adoption is governed by property law since embryos are considered to be property and not people in the United States. Once these contracts are signed by both the placing and adopting families, the adopting family now "owns" the embryos and the placing family has terminated all of their rights and responsibilities to the embryos.

The next step is for the adopting mother to work with her fertility clinic of choice to prepare her womb for a frozen embryo transfer (FET). Together, the couple and their doctor determine how many embryos to thaw and transfer into her womb for an attempt at pregnancy. Usually the number of embryos transferred is one, two, or three maximum. Hopefully after the FET, one or more of the embryos will implant itself in the uterine lining and continue the natural biological path to birth.

When the embryo-adopted child is born, the law of the United States says the woman who gives birth to the child is the child's legal mother, and the man to whom she is legally married is the child's legal father, and their names will be placed on the birth certificate. No formal court finalizations are necessary, but sometimes embryo-adopting families optionally choose to finalize their adoption in court.

As of 2016 there are eight embryo-adoption organizations in the U.S. More than 1,000 babies have been born as a result of the services provided by them. When choosing an embryo adoption organization, couples will want to clearly understand the program requirements and parameters. Some will give priority in matching to the placing family, some to the adopting family. Some will require a home study, some do not. As with any service provider it is important to understand if the program will give you the services most important to you.

While the Streges are thrilled to have been the first family to adopt an embryo, they want to make clear the whole program was orchestrated by God. "We give HIM all the glory and credit," reflects Marlene. "We could see God's fingerprints throughout our story and still do to this day."

Clockwise from top left: Hannah, eight months; Hannah, seventeen years; Hannah with Strege family friend, ESPN's Chris Mortensen; Hannah, current photo.

CHAPTER SIXTEEN

THE ULTIMATE ADOPTION STORY: JESUS OF NAZARETH

Now the birth of Jesus Christ took place in this way. When his mother Mary had been betrothed to Joseph, before they came together she was found to be with child from the Holy Spirit. And her husband Joseph, being a just man and unwilling to put her to shame, resolved to divorce her quietly. But as he considered these things, behold, an angel of the Lord appeared to him in a dream, saying, "Joseph, son of David, do not fear to take Mary as your wife, for that which is conceived in her is from the Holy Spirit. She will bear a son, and you shall call his name Jesus, for he will save his people from their sins." All this took place to fulfill what the Lord had spoken by the prophet: "Behold, the virgin shall conceive and bear a son, and they shall call his name Immanuel" (which means, God with us). When Joseph woke from sleep, he did as the angel of the Lord commanded him: he took his wife, but knew her not until she had given birth to a son. And he called his name Jesus. (Matthew 1:18–25)

The late Dr. Norman Vincent Peale, the longtime pastor of Marble Collegiate Church and bestselling author of dozens of books, once told the story of standing on the corner of 5th Avenue and 57th Street just a few days before Christmas. Along with two friends, one of whom was the late Fulton Oursler, the senior editor of *Reader's Digest*, the three men were attempting to hail a taxicab at rush hour. The traffic was horrendous, and the sidewalks were overflowing with people. Surveying the mayhem of shoppers streaming from store to store with their arms full of packages, Fulton spoke up.

"Isn't it something," he remarked. "A baby, born in a little village, thousands of miles away, two thousand years ago, is causing a traffic jam in New York City?" He then added, punching the air for emphasis, "What a baby!"

"Yes, indeed," Dr. Peale offered ponderously, "He's changed civilization."

"That isn't the best thing he did," the other friend replied. "He had a far tougher job. He changed *me*. He changed my life."[1]

Of course, it's one thing for three Christians to state the impact of Jesus on the world, but how about skeptics or critics of the faith? The late writer and historian H. G. Wells, an avowed atheist, once similarly referred to the impact of Jesus on the world. "I am a historian, I am not a believer," he wrote. "But I must confess as a historian that this penniless preacher from Nazareth is irrevocably the very center of history. Jesus Christ is easily the most dominant figure in all history."[2]

THE PART OF THE GREATEST STORY RARELY TOLD

The Christmas story is likely the most well-known and most often read story of all time. Each December, we read it from the Gospels of either Luke or Matthew in our churches and in our homes. Beginning before even Halloween, we see the Nativity depicted and displayed in various art forms, from cards to calendars and everywhere in between. Trees, twinkling lights, carols, and even stage performances featuring young children highlight the grandest of all miracles—the almost inconceivable story that

God would send His only Son to earth in the form of an innocent and helpless baby.

Indeed, whether you believe in the Incarnation or instead think it's a fable void of fact, the birth of Jesus Christ—the greatest story ever told about the greatest man who ever lived—has become a very familiar and world-changing narrative.

So, that is the story of Christmas and the holiday we celebrate each December.

But it's not nearly the entire story.

What is perhaps less discussed or considered is the fact that what follows the birth of Jesus on that starlit night in Bethlehem over two millennia ago is not just a made-for-Hallmark moment.

Instead, what follows is the most famous adoption story of all time.

JOSEPH WAS CHOSEN

When it comes to Jesus' adoptive father, Joseph, we only know about him what the Scriptures tell us—and the Bible doesn't tell us very much.

We know Joseph was a direct descendant of King David (Luke 1:27). This fact is no small thing because it establishes Jesus, as the son of Joseph, to one day grow up and inherit the royal right to be king. From Matthew's Gospel, we learn Joseph was a carpenter (Matthew 13:55). How old was he at the time of Jesus' birth? It's impossible to know. Prior to the seventeenth century, Joseph was often depicted as an older man, but those depictions were merely speculative in nature. We don't know when Joseph was born—or when he died.

From the Christmas story, we learn Joseph was "pledged"—or engaged—to a virgin named Mary (Luke 1:27). When he was told she was pregnant, news that undoubtedly came as the shock and heartbreak of his life, he decided to quietly seek a divorce because he was "unwilling to put her to shame" (Matthew 1:19). Shortly thereafter, however, we learn Joseph had a remarkable dream containing very specific instructions from an angel.

"Joseph, son of David," the angel told him. "Do not fear to take Mary as your wife, for that which is conceived in her is from the Holy Spirit. She will bear a son, and you shall call his name Jesus, for he will save his people from their sins" (Matthew 1:20–21).

Upon waking, Joseph was convinced and convicted. He decided to marry Mary after all, and upon the birth of her baby, the couple, being obedient to the angel's decree, named Him Jesus (Luke 1:31, Matthew 1:25). In doing so, Joseph was adopting Mary's son and extending him all the rights and privileges of his family's royal heritage.

Jesus was the adoptive son of Joseph, but in the eyes of God and the law, Jesus was now one of his very own.

THE ADOPTIVE ADVENTURE

As each of the previous stories in this book have demonstrated, adoption is rarely, if ever, a neat and tidy thing. That's because adoption involves the fate of human life—the world's most valuable treasure. Whether a child comes from Russia or Richmond, Virginia, bundled inside the body of a baby is unquantifiable and immeasurable potential. God is the author of all life—but it's the free will of man that determines what kind of life a child will enjoy—or endure.

In the case of Jesus of Nazareth, we know King Herod was alarmed to learn of His arrival, a fact that led to a dramatic development and displacement in the young child's life.

"After Jesus was born in Bethlehem in Judea, during the time of King Herod, Magi from the east came to Jerusalem and asked, 'Where is the one who has been born king of the Jews?'" writes Matthew. "'We saw his star when it rose and have come to worship him.' When King Herod heard this he was disturbed, and all Jerusalem with him" (Matthew 2:1–4).

How could a tiny baby threaten a king as secure as Herod? According to historians, Herod wasn't very secure at all. Actually, he was paranoid. By the time Jesus came along, Herod had been on the throne for nearly three decades and spent the vast majority of those years protecting his position. Any perceived threat—real or otherwise—was dealt with immediately and often with deadly force. At various points of his reign, he believed members of his own family were plotting to overthrow him. In response, he had his mother-in-law and three of his own sons, including his favored firstborn son, Antipater, executed. So, when the Magi appeared on the scene seeking to meet the new "King of the Jews," it's little wonder the current "King of the Jews"—Herod—would want to take decisive action.

As Matthew reported:

> Then Herod summoned the wise men secretly and ascertained from them what time the star had appeared. And he sent them to Bethlehem, saying, "Go and search diligently for the child, and when you have found him, bring me word, that I too may come and worship him." (Matthew 2:7–8)

As we know, Herod had no interest in worshiping Jesus but instead wanted to vanquish Him as a threat and have the baby killed. We learn the Magi were warned in a dream not to go back to Herod but to return via another route, which they did (Matthew 2:12). At the same time, an angel appeared to Joseph and advised him to leave Israel and escape to Egypt with Mary and Jesus (Matthew 2:13). When the King learned of the Magi's escape, he became furious and ordered all the male children of the region who were two years old or under to be killed (Matthew 2:16). This episode is often referred to as the "Massacre of the Innocents."

MODERN-DAY PARALLELS

The drama of the biblical scene is both breathtaking and heartbreaking. In fact, it's a far cry from the idyllic picture so often painted in our minds of a "silent night" in a peaceful straw-strewn stable. Indeed, all might have been "calm" and "bright" on the night of Jesus' birth—but it wasn't long before the tranquil scene of Mary, Joseph, and Jesus neatly tucked in together on a cold winter's night nearly turned tragic.

Just picture a blood-thirsty king and his henchmen in desperate search of a baby and his family—all with the expressed intent to murder the newborn as soon as they locate him. His mother and father bundle him up in blankets, perhaps even hiding the very child who represents "the hopes and fears of all the years"[3] in a basket or a bucket as they frantically make their exit to a foreign land.

It's hardly a charming and glamorous story. It's anything but, actually.

In fact, it's the personification of dysfunction.

It's gritty.

It's mystery, mayhem, and chaos all wrapped up in one.

In other words, in so many ways, it's a classic adoption story.

Yet, when it comes to God's sovereignty, it's critical we remember there is no such thing as plan B. "I make known the end from the beginning, from ancient times, what is still to come," God declares in the book of Isaiah. "I say, 'My purpose will stand, and I will do all that I please'" (Isaiah 46:10).

MAN CANNOT THWART GOD'S PURPOSES

That God chose to have His only Son enter the world through the womb of a young and impoverished unwed mother—in a stable surrounded by foul-smelling animals—makes little sense to us. That is, it makes little sense until we stand back and try to see His larger story.

The unconventional circumstances surrounding Jesus' birth and adoption serve to remind us that God's purposes are far bigger than our own. Why He chooses to do what He does—and when—is something that's part of a larger story often beyond our feeble and finite comprehension. Just because something doesn't make sense to us doesn't necessarily mean it doesn't make sense. Since the beginning of time, this truth has frustrated and confused even the most hardened believer. Yet, as the Dutch theologian Abraham Kuyper once famously stated, "There is not a square inch in the whole domain of our human existence over which Christ, who is Sovereign over all, does not cry, 'Mine!'"[4]

OUR ADOPTION IN CHRIST

It's in Joseph's adoption of Jesus that God chooses to demonstrate and illustrate a fundamental fact of our Christian faith. If we want to better understand our relationship with our Father in Heaven, we would be wise to better understand the very nature of adoption itself.

When a child is adopted, they're granted the same rights and privileges a biological child enjoys with his or her blood relatives. Mind you, they did nothing to earn this right—they were simply granted it by both the power of the law and the generosity and graciousness of the adoptive parents.

This same rationale explains the foundation of our relationship with Jesus.

It was the Gospel writer John who wrote, "But to all who did receive him, who believed in his name, he gave the right to become children of God, who were *born*, not of blood nor of the will of the flesh nor of the will of man, but of God" (John 1:12–13). The apostle Paul further emphasized the special adoptive relationship we have with Jesus Christ when he wrote to the church at Galatia.

"But when the fullness of time had come, God sent forth his Son, born of woman, born under the law, to redeem those who were under the law, so that we might receive adoption as sons" (Galatians 4:4–5).

You might have been reading this book and thinking you had little in common with those profiled. Think again. For those who claim Christ as their personal Lord and Savior, regardless of your family of origin—you're adopted. And as a member of Christ's family, you receive all the rights and privileges that accompany such an intimate relationship.

The apostle Paul makes this abundantly clear in his letter to the Romans when he wrote, "For all who are led by the Spirit of God are sons of God. For you did not receive the spirit of slavery to fall back into fear, but you have received the Spirit of adoption as sons, by whom we cry, 'Abba! Father!' The Spirit himself bears witness with our spirit that we are children of God, and if children, then heirs—heirs of God and fellow heirs with Christ, provided we suffer with him in order that we may also be glorified with him" (Romans 8:14–17).

The late Jerry Bridges nicely summed up this reality when he observed, "A son or daughter in any human family is either born to or adopted by the parents. By definition, a child can't be both. But with God we're both born of Him and adopted by Him."[5]

JOSEPH'S DECISION CHANGED THE WORLD

It would be easy to gloss over Joseph's decision to say "yes" to the adoption of Jesus as something of a fait accompli. After all, in His sovereignty, God knew how he'd answer long before the question was even asked. Yet, like all of us, Joseph still had the freedom to say "no." He didn't, of course, but such is the human story. Every day we're faced with significant decisions—many of which carry eternal consequences.

"Joseph stood by Mary and her expected child, and he cared for them as they trudged the weary way to Bethlehem," writes the British theologian and physicist John Polkinghorne. "After the birth there comes another disturbing message. Herod is seeking the child to take his life. Instantly and decisively, Joseph acts, hastening the family to safety in Egypt. How different the Christmas story would have been without the rock-solid faithfulness of Joseph."[6]

That so little is known about Joseph outside of the birth story of Jesus is a matter of great curiosity and even speculation. When last we hear of the carpenter, Jesus is just twelve years old. It's the Festival of the Passover, and the family is returning home from Jerusalem. After traveling for an entire day, Joseph and Mary realize Jesus is not with them (Luke 21:43). They return to Jerusalem and find him teaching and asking questions of the elders in the Temple. We're told that everyone who heard him were "amazed at his understanding and his answers" (Luke 21:47).

After they've been reunited, Luke records a rather terse exchange between Jesus and His mother. "Son, why have you treated us so?" she asks. "Behold, your father and I have been searching for you in great distress" (Luke 21:48). Jesus responds with indignation. "Why were you looking for me? Did you not know that I must be in my Father's house?" (Luke 21:49).

Jesus' answer reminds us that in God's economy, our relationship with our Heavenly Father must take precedence over our relationship with everyone else, including our earthly parents—biological or adoptive. He wasn't diminishing Joseph's or Mary's role or their importance. In fact, Luke further records Jesus returned with them to Nazareth and was "submissive" to their leadership (Luke 21:51). He's acknowledging and respecting the authority His parents have over Him (Ephesians 6:1).

Jesus' response might also provide comforting perspective for all those who struggle with unresolved parental relationships. For the individual who has been adopted and wonders in the still of the night about their birth parents—or perhaps for those who are estranged from or struggling with their biological parents—Jesus' words communicate a simple but profound truth. In the words of Peter, we're all "sojourners and exiles" just passing through. As this book has hopefully demonstrated, our earthly relationships matter. They have consequences for generations. But in the end, it's our relationship with Jesus that matters most of all.

JOSEPH'S OBSCURITY—JESUS' PROMINENCE

Following the incident in the temple, we never hear about Joseph again. As such, there seems to be consensus the adoptive father of Jesus died sometime between when He was twelve and thirty years of age. He's never referenced in the midst of Jesus' three-year ministry—only His mother is noted as being at the wedding at Cana (John 2:3) and at the crucifixion, Jesus asks John to care for Mary, an indication Joseph was no longer alive (John 19:26–27).

Is it possible to draw anything from Joseph's obscurity? Is it significant that as Joseph fades from the pages of Scripture, Jesus rises in prominence, both figuratively and ultimately, literally? After Jesus' birth, even Mary appears to play a rather silent role in the life and ministry of Jesus.

This is not to diminish the critical role both Joseph and Mary played in the raising of God's only Son, a child who was both fully human and fully divine. Instead, could it be God is trying to get across the fact adoption is primarily about meeting the needs of the child who is being adopted as opposed to tending to the comfort of the adoptive parents?

A FINAL WORD

"It is important to realize we adopt not because we are rescuers," writes David Platt, an adoptive father who currently serves as the president of the Southern Baptist Convention's International Mission Board. "No. We adopt because we are rescued."[7]

This is why the birth story of Jesus is the ultimate adoption story and one that foreshadows our own adoption in Him.

> For God so loved the world that he gave his one and only Son, that whoever believes in him shall not perish but have eternal life (John 3:16).

AFTERWORD

s a young boy growing up in Brooklyn, I loved to ask questions. In fact, my friends nicknamed me "Larry the Mouthpiece"—a nod to my love of radio and my hobby of calling Brooklyn Dodgers' games into a rolled-up scorecard from the Ebbets Field bleachers.

After the game, my friends would chase down the players for autographs. I didn't want any autographs. Instead, I wanted to ask the players questions.

"Why did you bunt, Pee Wee?"

"Duke, about that home run in the fifth inning—was it a curveball or a slider?"

Even as a kid at an early age, I realized that I never learned anything when I was talking. I already knew what I thought—I wanted to know what the other guy was thinking.

This combination of a love of radio and a fierce spirit of curiosity led me in 1957 to my first on-air job at WAHR-AM in Miami, Florida. I was a disc jockey. A year later, I was hosting a live radio interview show on WIOD at Pumpernik's Restaurant in Miami Beach. I'd strike up a conversation with anyone who walked in the door. My first guest was a waiter. A few days later, I was interviewing the famed singer Bobby Darin.

Nearly sixty years later, I've conducted over sixty thousand interviews. I've spoken with people from all walks of life—everyone from clerics to criminals, heads of state to sports celebrities and lots of Hollywood legends.

I've loved every minute of it—because I love people and find them interesting—because I'm interested in them. I especially enjoy finding out what makes people tick and what makes them successful.

Which is why I'm eager to introduce you to the stories in *Chosen for Greatness: How Adoption Changes the World.*

I wasn't adopted—but I've interviewed nearly all of the people Paul Batura has chosen to highlight in this book. They include Apple's Steve Jobs, Nancy Reagan, Nelson Mandela, President Gerald Ford, Art Linkletter, Faith Hill, Newt Gingrich, and Scott Hamilton.

I've sat across the table from all of them—and I've learned something from all of them, too.

Being a huge baseball fan, I wish I could have sat down with the Babe, but he passed away a decade before I began my career.

I think you'll find in these pages the same spirit of curiosity that I've tried to make the hallmark of my own shows. From my early days in radio to CNN's *Larry King Live!* and now *Larry King Now* on Ora TV, I've discovered that everyone is interesting—if you're willing to ask good questions.

Every child deserves someone to love and cherish them—and every child in this book succeeded because someone chose to invest in them through adoption and foster care.

I've made a career asking questions, so let me close by posing one to you:

If there's a child out there looking for a parent—could that someone be you?

Larry King
Los Angeles, CA
September 2016

AUTHOR'S NOTE AND ACKNOWLEDGMENTS

By now you have recognized that a common theme threaded throughout the pages of this book is that all of us, whether we were adopted or raised by our biological parents, are the product of the lives that have touched ours. The road to success may sometimes seem lonely, but those who reach its end never travel alone. Assistance can come in many forms and over the course of many years. Surely this is the case with *Chosen for Greatness*.

For her unceasing encouragement, counsel, insight, wisdom, patience and devotion, my wife and best friend, Julie, is deserving of the highest praise. Marrying an aspiring and sometimes frustrated writer and then parenting young children is not for the faint of heart, but especially when your husband is holed away for hours each day working on a manuscript. Our children, Riley, Will, and Alex are constant reminders of the precious gift of adoption. When I open this book in the coming years, I'll forever recall our boys playfully and happily barging into my home office, inquiring on its progress—always with a smile and a twinkle in their eyes. Without their birth mothers, Julianna, Joli, and Jennifer, respectively, I would not have received the inspiration to attempt to inspire others with the incredible stories inside these pages. Simply thanking a birth parent for entrusting you with their child seems wholly inadequate when compared to the magnitude of the decision. Theirs is truly an "indescribable gift."

While working on this project, I often thought about my late mother, Joan Cummings Batura, the woman who first inspired me to write because I saw how much she loved to read. I bless her memory. My father, Jim Batura, prayed for me and this project, as did my in-laws, Reverend Jennings and Cindy Hamilton. Those prayers were felt and are most appreciated.

My dear friend, Bob DeMoss, one of the most talented writers and storytellers of our time, a man who first believed in this project and helped bring it to life, is worthy of special recognition. Everyone should have a "Bobby D" in their life. Special thanks also to my friend and agent, Erik Wolgemuth.

I want to thank several people who have invested in me as a writer. Over the years my colleagues at Focus on the Family have entrusted countless writing projects to my care. Their confidence in me and their skillful editing have shaped and developed my abilities. These include Focus president Jim Daly, the ministry's chief of staff, Joel Vaughan, and my friend Ron Reno. It would be impossible to overstate how much I have learned about writing from the founder of Focus, Dr. James Dobson. For ten years I served as his research assistant and watched up close and personal how much care and devotion he put into his writings. I would like to think he helped teach me a bit how to tell a story in a compelling, efficient, and enjoyable way. When it comes to advocating for children in search of a forever home, the team at Focus' Wait No More program has inspired me. Led by my friends Kelly Rosati and Dr. Sharen Ford, they serve as humble champions of life. I applaud them and their work.

Librarians at the Pikes Peak Library were indispensable as I pored through biographies, periodicals, and journals. There are few places where our tax dollars are better spent and less heralded than the public library.

Last but certainly not least, I would like to express my gratitude to the great team at Regnery Faith. Led by publisher Marji Ross, editor-in-chief Gary Terashita, and copy editors Kristin Jaroma and Maria Ruhl, these exceptional individuals are passionate about their books, and they know how to make things happen. This is my third title with them, and I'm already looking forward to the fourth.

As noted in chapter fourteen, Johann Sebastian Bach wrote the letters "SDG"—"For the Glory of God Alone"—at the bottom of every page of his compositions. If it were practical to do so in this book, I would like to do the same. That's because books are just books—they are conceived, composed, and (hopefully) read. Even a bestseller today is soon sold for twenty-five cents down at Goodwill. So this project will have been a complete waste of time if the reader doesn't conclude that it is not human accomplishment that truly makes man great. Instead, it is the greatness of God—breathed into the body and soul of every human being—freely available for those who will receive it—that makes life—and the lives of these featured—great and worth living.

SDG!

Will   Alex   Riley

NOTES

EPIGRAPH

1. Malcolm Gladwell, *Outliers* (New York: Little Brown & Co., 2008), 18.
2. Reverend Richard Halverson (1916–1995), former United States Senate Chaplain and senior pastor of the Fourth Presbyterian Church in Bethesda, Maryland, Dr. Halverson famously offered these words as a benediction at the conclusion of every service.
3. See: "Why You Should Consider Adoption," https://www.thegospelcoalition.org/article/why-you-should-consider-adoption.

INTRODUCTION: ON THE VERGE OF EVERYTHING

1. Benson Bobrick, *Angel in the Whirlwind* (New York: Simon and Schuster, 1997).
2. Henry David Thoreau, *Walden* (New York: F. Watts, 1969).

CHAPTER ONE: STEVE JOBS

1.   Walter Isaacson, *Steve Jobs* (New York: Simon and Schuster, 2011), 15.
2.   Ibid., 6.
3.   Ibid., 6.
4.   Ibid., 6–7.
5.   Ibid., 9.
6.   Karen Blumenthal, see: http://us.macmillan.com/mobile/excerpt/9781250015570
7.   "Heathkits" were electronic products produced by the Heath Company.
8.   Isaacson, *Steve Jobs*, 16.
9.   Ibid., 7, 125.
10. Ibid., 17.
11. Ibid., 4.
12. Ibid.
13. Ibid., 5.
14. Ibid.
15. Ibid., 245.
16. "A Sister's Eulogy for Steve Jobs," see: http://newsroom.ucla.edu/stories/a-sister-s-eulogy-for-steve-jobs-220058.
17. Ibid.

CHAPTER TWO: NANCY REAGAN

1.   Anne Edwards, see: http://catdir.loc.gov/catdir/samples/hol051/2003046684.html.
2.   Michelle Green, "A Find at a Flea Market Sheds Lights on Nancy Reagan's Life with Real Father," *People*, 18 July 1983. See: http://www.people.com/people/archive/article/0,,20085496,00.html.
3.   Kitty Kelly, *Nancy Reagan: The Unauthorized Biography* (New York: Simon and Schuster, 1991).
4.   Ibid.
5.   Nancy Reagan, *My Turn: The Memoirs of Nancy Reagan* (New York: Random House, 1989).
6.   Ibid.
7.   Nancy Reagan, Ibid.

8. Ibid.

9. Ibid.

10. Kitty Kelly, Ibid.

11. Ibid.

12. Bob Colacello, *Ronnie & Nancy: Their Path to the White House, 1911–1980* (New York: Warner Books, 2004), 35.

13. Nancy Reagan, Ibid.

14. Colacello, Ibid., 38.

15. Nancy Reagan, Ibid.

16. Jennie Sweetman, "Nancy Reagan's Connection to Sussex County," *New Jersey Herald*, 24 April, 2016. See: http://www.njherald.com/article/20160424/ARTICLE/304249987#

17. Peggy Noonan, *What I Saw at the Revolution: A Political Life in the Reagan Era* (New York: Random House, 1990), 59.

18. Howard Rosenberg, "Ronald Reagan's Farewell: The Power and the Glory," *Los Angeles Times*, 17 August 1988.

19. Lou Cannon, "Nancy Reagan, Influential and Protective First Lady, Dies at 94," *New York Times*, 6 March 2016. See: http://www.nytimes.com/2016/03/07/us/nancy-reagan-a-stylish-and-influential-first-lady-dies-at-94.html?_r=0.

CHAPTER THREE: NELSON MANDELA

1. David Beresford, "Nelson Mandela Obituary," *The Guardian*, 5 December 2013. See: https://www.theguardian.com/world/2013/dec/05/nelson-mandela-obituary.

2. Bill Keller, "Nelson Mandela, South Africa's Liberator as Prisoner and President, Dies at 95," *New York Times*, 5 December 2013. See: http://www.nytimes.com/2013/12/06/world/africa/nelson-mandela_obit.html?pagewanted=all.

3. Statement by former President George H. W. Bush on the death of former South African President Nelson Mandela, 5 December 2013. See: https://www.facebook.com/georgebush41/photos/pb.285998961428260.-2207520000.1461689893./735616866466465/?type=3&theater.

4. "Nelson Mandela: Jacob Zuma says, 'Our Nation has Lost Its Greatest Son," BBC News, 6 December 2013. See: http://www.bbc.com/news/world-africa-25248713.

5. "Democracy Owes Mandela 'Vast, Lasting Debt," News24, 6 December 2013. See: http://www.news24.com/SouthAfrica/News/Democracy-owes-Mandela-vast-lasting-debt-20131206.

6. Martin Meredith, *Mandela: A Biography* (New York: St. Martin's Press, 1998), 5.

7. Nelson Mandela, *Long Walk to Freedom: The Autobiography of Nelson Mandela* (Boston: Little, Brown, 1994), 39.

8. Ibid. See: http://www.pbs.org/wgbh/pages/frontline/shows/mandela/boy/book.html.

9. David Beresford, Ibid.

10. Mandela, Ibid., 20–21.

11. Ibid.

12. Ibid.

13. Ibid.

14. Ibid.

15. Ibid.

16. Ibid.

17. Tom Hiney, *On the Missionary Trail: A Journey Through Polynesia, Asia, and Africa with the London Missionary Society* (New York: Atlantic Monthly Press, 2000), 333.

18. Mandela, Ibid., 18.

19. Ibid., 18.

20. Ibid., 19.

21. Ibid., 19.

22. Ibid.

23. Ibid.

24. Mac Maharaj, Ahmad M. Kathrada, Mandela: The Authorized Portrait (Kansas City, MO: Andrews McMeel Pub., 2006).

25. Mandela, Ibid.

26. Ibid.

27. Ibid., see: https://books.google.com/books?id=RHwLqVrnXgIC&pg=PT27&lpg=PT27&dq=%E2%80%9Cand+I+did+not+want+to+appear+to+be+a+fraud+in+the+eyes+of+my+fellow+students.%E2%8

0%9D&source=bl&ots=V2ZBzo3VvM&sig=lxl-tx8jeXW_STKNZ
5dBAM5jeIQ&hl=en&sa=X&ved=0ahUKEwjF4pLn0I7OAhUJ7o
MKHUbnAVkQ6AEIHDAA#v=onepage&q=%E2%80%9C
and%20I%20did%20not%20want%20to%20appear%20to%20
be%20a%20fraud%20in%20the%20eyes%20of%20my%20
fellow%20students.%E2%80%9D&f=false.

28. Ibid., see: https://books.google.com/books?id=RHwLqVrnXgIC&p
g=PT32&dq=but+it+was+actually+the+very+beginning+of+a+much
+longer+and+more+trying+journey+that+would+test+me+in+ways+t
hat+I+could+not&hl=en&sa=X&ved=0ahUKEwiunsij0Y7OAhUl5I
MKHVY_DKcQ6AEIHjAA#v=onepage&q=but%20it%20
was%20actually%20the%20very%20beginning%20of%20a%20
much%20longer%20and%20more%20trying%20journey%20
that%20would%20test%20me%20in%20ways%20that%20I%20
could%20not&f=false.

29. Ibid.

30. Nelson Mandela, International Defence and Aid Fund, I Am
Prepared to Doe (London: Christian Action Publications Ltd.,
1970), 23.

31. See: "Nelson Mandela, in His Words," *Wall Street Journal*, 5
December 2013. http://www.wsj.com/articles/SB100014241278873
2394990457857294290182734

32. 32 Lydia Polgreen, John Eligon, Alan Cowell, "Thousands Gather
to Bury Mandela in His Home Village, *The New York Times*, 15
December 2013. See: http://www.nytimes.com/2013/12/16/world/
africa/nelson-mandela-funeral.html?pagewanted=all.

CHAPTER FOUR: BABE RUTH

1. Babe Ruth, Bob Considine, The Babe Ruth Story (New York: E.P.
Dutton, 1948), George Roy, Steven Hilliard Stern, Live Schreiber,
"Babe Ruth," HBO's Sports of the 20th Century, Black Canyon
Productions, New York, New York, 1998.

2. Robert W. Creamer, *Babe Ruth: The Legend Comes to Life* (New
York: Simon and Schuster, 1974), 37.

3. Leigh Montville, *The Big Bam: The Life and Times of Babe Ruth*
(New York: Doubleday, 2006), 14.

4.   Marshall Smelser, *The Life That Ruth Built: A Biography* (Lincoln, NE: University of Nebraska Press, 1975), 7.

5.   Creamer, Ibid., 38.

6.   Montville, Ibid., 36.

7.   George Herman Ruth, "Babe Ruth on the Foundation of Faith," *Guideposts*, October 1948. See: https://www.guideposts.org/positive-living/paths-to-fulfillment/encouragement/guideposts-classics-babe-ruth-on-the-foundation?nopaging=1

8.   Smelser, Ibid., 26.

9.   George Herman Ruth, "Babe Ruth on the Foundation of Faith," Ibid.

10.   Ibid.

11.   Montville, Ibid., 25.

12.   See: http://entertainment.howstuffworks.com/babe-ruth3.htm

13.   Montville, Ibid., 35.

14.   Brother Gilbert, C.F.X., Harry Rothgerber, Young Babe Ruth: His Early Life and Baseball Career, from the Memoirs of a Xaverian Brother (Jefferson, N.C.:McFarland & Co., 1999), 4.

15.   George Roy, Steven Hilliard Stern, Live Schreiber, "Babe Ruth," HBO's Sports of the 20th Century, Ibid.

16.   Babe Ruth Quotes, see: http://www.baseball-almanac.com/quotes/quoruth.shtml.

17.   George Herman Ruth, "Babe Ruth on the Foundation of Faith," Ibid.

18.   Ibid.

19.   Ibid.

20.   Ibid.

21.   Smelser, Ibid, 34.

CHAPTER FIVE: JOHN HANCOCK

1.   Charles Francis, *Wisdom Well Said: Anecdotes, Fables, Legends, Myths, Humor and Wise Sayings that Capture the Human Condition* (El Prado, NM: Levine Mesa Press, 2006), 214.

2.   "Signers of the Declaration of Independence," see: http://www.ushistory.org/declaration/signers/hancock.html

3. Herbert S. Allen, John Hancock: Patriot in Purple (New York: MacMillan and Co., 1948), iii.

4. Ibid.

5. William Parsons, *Two discourses, delivered September 29, 1839, on occasion of the two hundredth anniversary of the gathering of the First Congregational church, Quincy: with an appendix* (Boston: J. Munroe and Company, 1840), 47.

6. Ebenzer Gay, *The Untimely Death of a Man of God Lamented: In a Sermon Preach'd at the Funeral of the Reverend Mr. John Hancock, Pastor of the First Church of Christ in Braintree ; who died May 7th. 1744* (Boston: Printed by S. Kneeland and T. Green in Queen-Street), 19.

7. Ibid., 6.

8. Ibid., 19.

9. S. E. Morison, *Three Centuries of Harvard: 1636-1936* (Cambridge, MA: Harvard University Press, 19360, 103.

10. 10 John Hancock Mutual Life Insurance Company, John Hancock: Great American Patriot (Boston: The Company, 1927), 2.

11. *The Times-Picayune*, 13 July 1880, 2.

12. Allen, Ibid.

13. "John Hancock's Boston Massacre Oration," 5 March 1744. See: http://law2.umkc.edu/faculty/projects/ftrials/bostonmassacre/hancockoration.html

14. James Spear Loring, *The Hundred Boston Orators Appointed by the Municipal Authorities and other Public Bodies, from 1770 to 1852; Comprising Historical Gleanings Illustrating the Principles and Progress of Our Republican Institutions* (Boston: J.P. Jewett, 1853), 120.

15. *The Independent Chronicle*, 10 October 1793.

16. John Adams, Francis Adams, The Works of John Adams, Second President of the United States, Vol. 10 (Boston, Little, Brown, 1850-56), 261.

CHAPTER SIX: DAVE THOMAS

1.   Franklin Delano Roosevelt, "Address Accepting the Presidential Nomination at the Democratic National Convention in Chicago," 2 July 1932. See: http://www.presidency.ucsb.edu/ws/?pid=75174.

2.   Dave Thomas, *Well Done! The Common Guy's Guide to Everyday Success* (Grand Rapids, MI: Zondervan, 1994), 20.

3.   Marilyn Achiron, "Dave Thomas," People Magazine, 2 August 1993. See: http://www.people.com/people/archive/article/0,,20105985,00.html.

4.   Edward F. Bland, M.D., "Rheumatic Fever: The Way it Was," AHA Journal, December, 1987, 1190-1195. See: http://circ.ahajournals.org/content/circulationaha/76/6/1190.full.pdf.

5.   Ibid.

6.   Claire Mencke, "Dave Thomas, The Beef Behind Winner Wendy's," Investor's Business Daily, 15 June 2015. See: http://www.investors.com/news/management/leaders-and-success/dave-thomas-built-wendys-into-a-winner/.

7.   Ibid.

8.   Jeff Louderback, Wendy's Dave Thomas Profile," Ohio Magazine. See: http://www.jefflouderback.com/dave-thomas-profile-for-ohio-magazine/.

9.   R. David Thomas, *Dave's Way* (New York: Berkley Books, 1991), 11-12.

10.   Marilyn Achiron, Ibid.

11.   R. David Thomas, *Dave's Way*, Ibid., 9-10.

12.   Dave Thomas, *Well Done!*, Ibid, 44.

13.   Marilyn Achiron, Ibid.

14.   Dave Thomas, *Well Done!*, Ibid, 31.

15.   Dave Thomas, "The Boss; Success of a Happy Man," *New York Times*, 5 April 2000. See: http://www.nytimes.com/2000/04/05/business/the-boss-success-of-a-happy-man.html.

16.   See: https://www.wendys.com/en-us/about-wendys/daves-legacy.

17.   Louderback, Ibid.

18.   Ibid.

19.   R. David Thomas, *Dave's Way*, Ibid., 31.

20.   Ibid., 33.

21. Louderback, Ibid.

22. Marilyn Achiron, Ibid.

23. Ibid.

24. Ibid.

25. Louderback, Ibid.

26. Statement from Steve Anderson, President and CEO of the National Restaurant Association on the Passing of Dave Thomas, 9 January 2002. See: http://www.just-food.com/news/statement-from-steven-c-anderson-president-ceo-of-the-national-restaurant-association-on-the-passing-of-dave-thomas_id74170.aspx.

27. "President Honors 2003 Presidential Medal of Freedom Recipients,"23 July 2003. See: https://georgewbush-whitehouse.archives.gov/news/releases/2003/07/20030723-9.html.

28. See: https://books.google.com/books?id=aPAwhOGUggQC&pg=PA320&lpg=PA320&dq=%E2%80%9CThere+is+no+question+Dave+Thomas+will+be+remembered+as+a+man+of+humble+beginnings+who+created+one+of+the+most+successful+fast-food+chains+in+the+entire+world%E2%80%9D&source=bl&ots=1PzK61NO_3&sig=X7mJMGVxHzrVeJ48Vw5wrouIVhE&hl=en&sa=X&ved=0ahUKEwiOkrrilZbOAhVrwYMKHQGSAZsQ6AEIHDAA#v=onepage&q=%E2%80%9CThere%20is%20no%20question%20Dave%20Thomas%20will%20be%20remembered%20as%20a%20man%20of%20humble%20beginnings%20who%20created%20one%20of%20the%20most%20successful%20fast-food%20chains%20in%20the%20entire%20world%E2%80%9D&f=false.

29. "Dave Thomas, Founder of Wendy's, Dies at 69," *New York Times*, 8 January 2002. See: http://www.nytimes.com/2002/01/08/obituaries/08WIRE-THOM.html.

30. Kim Foltz, "The Media Business: Advertising; At Wendy's, Folksiness is Effective," *New York Times*, 22 August 1990. See: http://www.nytimes.com/1990/08/22/business/the-media-business-advertising-at-wendy-s-folksiness-is-effective.html.

31. Sue Chastain, "A Hamburger Man, Plain And Simple Dave Thomas Loves His Work. Here To Plug A Book, He Seemed The Same Modest Guy He Is On TV," *Philadelphia Inquirer*, 3 November 1992. See: http://articles.philly.com/1992-11-03/.

living/26008574_1_college-education-hamburger-empire-national-adoption-center.

ADOPTION MILESTONES: THE RISE AND FALL OF ORPHANAGES

1.   Plato, *Laws* (Champaigne, Ill: Project Gutenberg, 1995), 927.
2.   Neil J. O'Connell, "George Whitefield and Bethesda Orphan House," *The Georgia Historical Quarterly*, Spring, 1970, 41-62. See: https://www.jstor.org/stable/40579041?seq=1#page_scan_tab_contents
3.   Marvin Olasky, "American Orphanages: How We Used to Care for Children," *Philanthropy, Culture and Society*, May 1996, 1-6.
4.   Dale Keiger, "The Rise and Demise of the American Orphanage," *Johns Hopkins Magazine*, July 2003. See: http://pages.jh.edu/jhumag/496web/orphange.html
5.   *Proceeding of the New Hampshire of Charities and Collections, 1909* (Concord, NH: Rumford Printing Co, 1909), 27.
6.   Keiger, Ibid.
7.   John M. Simmons, "I'd Rather Be in An Orphanage," see: http://johnmsimmons.com/id-rather-be-in-an-orphanage/.

CHAPTER SEVEN: ART LINKLETTER

1.   Gary Rotstein, "Aging Art Linkletter Says the Darndest Things," Post-Gazette, 8 October 1999. See: http://old.post-gazette.com/healthscience/19991008oldies2.asp
2.   "TV Host Art Linkletter Dies at 97," AP, 26 May 2010. See: http://www.today.com/popculture/tv-host-art-linkletter-dies-97-1C9400900
3.   Art Linkletter, *Confessions of a Happy Man* (New York: Random House, 1960), 16,
4.   Linkletter, Ibid. 31.
5.   Ibid, 15.
6.   Ibid.,18.
7.   Ibid.
8.   Ibid.
9.   Ibid., 16.
10.   Ibid., 19.

11. Ibid., 20.
12. Ibid., 22.
13. Ibid.
14. Art Linkletter, "Unwanted Baby Finds Parents," *Pittsburgh Post-Gazette*, 15 February 1961, 35.
15. Linkletter, Ibid., 23.
16. Ibid., 32.
17. Ibid., 50.
18. Ibid.
19. Personal Interview, 2 May 2016.
20. Myrna Oliver and Valerie J. Nelson, "Art Linkletter, broadcasting pioneer who created 'Kids Say the Darndest Things,' dies at 97," *Los Angeles Times*, 26 May 2010.
21. Personal Interview, 2 May 2016.
22. Ibid.
23. Ibid.
24. Linkletter, Ibid., 104-105.

CHAPTER EIGHT: GERALD FORD

1. James M. Cannon, *Time and Chance: Gerald Ford's Appointment with History* (New York: Harper Collins, 1994), 13.
2. *The Harvard Herald*, 7 September 1912.
3. Cannon, Ibid., 4.
4. Cannon, Ibid., 6.
5. Cannon, Ibid., 9.
6. James Cannon, *Gerald R. Ford: An Honorable Life* (Ann Arbor: University of Michigan Press, 2013), 44.
7. Cannon, *Time and Chance*, Ibid., 11.
8. Cannon, Ibid., 10.
9. Cannon, Ibid., 9.
10. Paul F. Boller, Presidential Diversions: Presidents at Play from George Washington to George W. Bush (Orlando: Harcourt: 2007), 293.
11. "Growing Up Grand: Michigan's Own Gerald R. Ford," The Gerald R. Ford Presidential Museum. See: https://www.fordlibrarymuseum.

gov/museum/exhibits/GROWING%20UP%20GRAND-%20
WEBSiTE/Pages/Ford'sLifeSubpages/HomeLife.html.

12. Cannon, *Time and Chance.*, Ibid, 15.

13. Joseph Rudyard Kipling, *Rewards and Fairies* (The University of Adelaide Library, 2009).

14. Blair H. Laackman, *Gerald R. Ford's Scouting Years* (Grand Rapids, MI: West Michigan Shores Council, 1982).

15. "Remarks at the Boy Scouts' Annual Awards Dinner," 2 December 1974, The American Presidency Project. See: http://www.presidency.ucsb.edu/ws/?pid=4601.

16. Cannon, *Time and Chance*, Ibid., 15.

17. Cannon, Ibid.

18. Cannon, *Gerald R. Ford: An Honorable Life.*, Ibid., 47.

19. Cannon, *Time and Chance*, Ibid., 14.

20. "President Gerald R. Ford Remarks on Taking Office," 9 August 1974, The History Place: Great Speeches Collection. See: http://www.historyplace.com/speeches/ford-sworn.htm.

21. Douglas Brinkley, Arthur M. Schlesinger., Jr., *Gerald R. Ford: The American President Series: The 38th President, 1974-1977* (New York: Times Books, 2007), 5.

22. Peggy Noonan, "Ford Without Tears," *Wall Street Journal*, 30 December 2006. See: http://www.wsj.com/articles/SB116742753817862742.

23. Ibid.

CHAPTER NINE: GEORGE WASHINGTON CARVER

1. Jason H. Gart, He Shall Direct Thy Paths: The Early Life of George Washington Carver (Midwest Regional Office, National Park Service, U.S. Department of the Interior, 2014), "Interview with Roy Porter," Slave Girl Mary, October 28, 1957, GWCNM Library; "Interview with Roy C. Porter,

2. William J. Federer, George Washington Carver: His Life and Faith in His Own Words (St. Louis, MO: Amerisearch, Inc., 2002), 39.

3. Ernie Pyle, David Nichols, *Ernie's America: The Best of Ernie Pyle's 1930's Travel Dispatches* (New York: Random House, 1989).

4. Federer, Ibid., 39.

5. Zachary Hutchins, "George Washington Carver: Advocate for Southern Farming," Documenting the American South. See: http://docsouth.unc.edu/highlights/carver.html.

6. Federer, Ibid., 29.

7. Laurie Johnston, "The Enshrinement of George Washington Carver; Hall of Fame Is Slated to Enshrine George Washington Carver Today," *New York Times*, 23 April 1977, 50.

8. Gary R. Kremer, *George Washington Carver: In His Own Words* (Columbia, MO: University of Missouri Press, 1987), 23.

9. Federer, Ibid., 27.

10. "The Foregoing Is a List of Written Questions Made Up by Raleigh H. Merritt, The Answers to Which Were Made by Dr. George W. Carver in His Own Hand Writing," July 1927, Reel 1, Frame 0022, Microfilm 17,416, The George Washington Carver Papers in the Tuskegee Institute Archives, Manuscript Division, Library of Congress.

11. William Joseph Federer, *America's God and Country: Encyclopedia of Quotations* (Coppell, TX: Fame, 1994), 97.

12. Kremer, Ibid., 11.

13. William J. Federer, *George Washington Carver: His Life and Faith in His Own Words*, Ibid., 67.

14. Linda McMurry Edwards, *Carver: Scientist and Symbol* (Oxford: Oxford University Press, 1981), 7.

15. Kremer, Ibid., 23.

16. William J. Federer, Ibid., 85.

17. Kremer, Ibid., 21.

18. John Perry, *George Washington Carver* (Nashville, TN: Thomas nelson, 2011), 8.

19. Christine Vella, *George Washington Carver: A Life* (Baton Rouge: Louisiana State University Press, 2015), 58.

20. George Washington Carver (Died 1943)

21. William J. Federer, *George Washington Carver: His Life and Faith in His Own Words*, Ibid., 53.

22. Ibid.

23. Editorial, *New York Times*, 20 November 1924.

24. Vella, Ibid., 196.

25. "Discovering George Washington Carver—A Man of Character," National Park Service: George Washington Carver National Monument, Diamond, MO. See: https://www.nps.gov/gwca/learn/education/upload/Charactor%20Education%20Book%20Grade%202.pdf.
26. "Notable Men in Black History," see: http://yakjam.com/notable-men-in-black-history/.

ADOPTION MILESTONES: RIDING THE RAILS TO TOMORROW

1. Phone interview; 30 June 2016.
2. Christina Baker Kline, *Orphan Train: A Novel* (New York: William Morrow, 2013).
3. National Orphan Train Complex History, see: http://orphantraindepot.org/history/

CHAPTER TEN: TOM MONAGHAN

1. Winston Churchill, "Christmas Message 1941," The Churchill Centre. See: http://www.winstonchurchill.org/resources/speeches/1941-1945-war-leader/802-christmas-message-1941
2. Ibid.
3. James Leonard, *Living the Faith: A Life of Tom Monaghan* (Ann Arbor: University of Michigan Press, 2012), 20.
4. Ibid.
5. Ibid., 19.
6. Tom Monaghan, *Pizza Tiger* (New York: Random House, 1986), 26.
7. Monaghan, Ibid., 26.
8. James Leonard, Ibid., 22.
9. Monaghan, Ibid., 26-27.
10. Monaghan, Ibid., 27.
11. Ibid.
12. Ibid., 29.
13. Ibid.
14. Ibid., 30.
15. Ibid., 30.
16. Ibid., 31.

17. Ibid.
18. Leonard, Ibid., 18.
19. Ibid., 27.
20. Leonard, Ibid., 28.
21. Monaghan, Ibid., 33.
22. Monaghan, Ibid., 34.
23. Leonard, Ibid., 30.
24. Monaghan, Ibid., 36.
25. Ibid.
26. Ibid., 37.
27. Ibid., 38.
28. Ibid., 38-39.
29. Ibid., 39
30. Ibid.
31. Ibid., 45.
32. C.S. Lewis, Mere Christianity (San Francisco: Harper Collins, 2009), 109.
33. Peter J. Boyer, "The Deliverer," *New Yorker*, 19 February 2007. See: http://www.newyorker.com/magazine/2007/02/19/the-deliverer.
34. Ibid.
35. Ibid.

CHAPTER ELEVEN: NEWT GINGRICH

1. Gail Sheehy, "The Inner Quest of Gail Sheehy," *Vanity Fair*, September 1995. See: http://www.pbs.org/wgbh/pages/frontline/newt/vanityfair1.html.
2. "The Long March of Newt Gingrich," PBS Frontline Show #1409, 16 January 1996. See: http://www.pbs.org/wgbh/pages/frontline/newt/newtscript.html.
3. William Douglas, "Newt Gingrich—A Portrait of a Complicated Politician," McClatchy Newspapers, 5 December 2011. See: http://www.mcclatchydc.com/news/politics-government/election/article24720061.html.
4. Sheehy, Ibid.
5. Sheehy, Ibid.

6. Newt Gingrich, *5 Principles for a Successful Life: From Our Family to Yours* (New York: Crown Forum, 2009), 39.

7. Sheehy., Ibid.

8. Tom Infield, "The PA Hamlet Where Young Gingrich Came of Age," *Philadelphia Inquirer*, 18 December 2011. See: http://articles. philly.com/2011-12-18/news/30531358_1_newt-gingrich-robert-gingrich-gingrich-connection.

9. Ibid.

10. Sandhya Somashekhar, "Gingrich Wild About Zoos," *Washington Post*, 9 December 2011. See: https://www.washingtonpost.com/ politics/2011/12/08/gIQAVb1yiO_story.html.

11. Mel Steely, *The Gentleman from Georgia: The Biography of Newt Gingrich* (Macon, GA: Mercer University Press, 2000), 4.

12. Sheehy, Ibid.

13. Gail Sheehy, "Newt Gingrich's Bipolar Mother Kit Gingrich and His Difficult Childhood," The Daily Beast, 11 December 2011. See: http://www.thedailybeast.com/articles/2011/12/22/newt-gingrich-s-bipolar-mother-kit-gingrich-and-his-difficult-childhood.html.

14. Sheehy, "The Inner Quest of Newt Gingrich," Ibid.

15. Steely, Ibid.

16. Elise Cooper, "Jackie Cushman on Her Dad," *American Thinker*, 24 December 2011. See: http://www.americanthinker.com/ articles/2011/12/jackie_gingrich_cushman_on_her_dad.html.

17. Steely, Ibid., 7.

18. Ibid., 8.

19. Mao Tse-tung (1893-1976).

20. Jeanne Cummings, "Gingrich Out to Save America," The Atlanta-Journal Constitution, 16 January 1994.

21. Steely, Ibid., 8.

22. Ibid., 9.

23. Sheehy, "The Inner Quest of Newt Gingrich," Ibid.

24. Ibid.

25. "Robert Gingrich; Retired Army Officer, Father of House Speaker, Associated Press, 21 November 1996. See: http://articles.latimes. com/1996-11-21/news/mn-1442_1_robert-gingrich.

26.   "Newt Gingrich Takes Gavel as First Republican House Speaker in 40 Years," NBC Today Show, 4 January 1994. See: https://archives.nbclearn.com/portal/site/k-12/flatview?cuecard=4919.

27.   Ibid.

28.   David Brody, "Newt Gingrich Tells The Brody File He 'Felt Compelled To Seek God's Forgiveness,'" CBN News, 8 March 2011. See: http://www1.cbn.com/thebrodyfile/archive/2011/03/08/newt-gingrich-tells-brody-file-he-felt-compelled-to-seek.

CHAPTER TWELVE: SCOTT HAMILTON

1.   Scott Hamilton, *Landing It: My Life On And Off The Ice* (New York: Kensington Books, 1999), 109.

2.   Ibid.

3.   Ibid., 106.

4.   Ibid., 18.

5.   Ibid., 19.

6.   Ibid.

7.   Ibid., 25.

8.   Ibid.

9.   Ibid.

10.   Ibid., 29.

11.   Ibid.

12.   Ibid., 30.

13.   Ibid., 33.

14.   Ibid., 42.

15.   Ibid.

16.   Ibid.,50.

17.   Ibid., 55.

18.   Ibid., 64.

19.   Ibid., 78.

20.   Ibid.

21.   Ibid.

22.   Ibid., 81.

23.   Ibid., 178.

24. Jayne Thurber-Smith, "Scott Hamilton: A Star On and Off the Ice," The Salvation Army, 29 April 2011. See: http://salvationist. ca/2011/04/scott-hamilton-a-star-on-and-off-ice/.

25. Hamilton., Ibid., 187-188.

26. Ibid., 184.

27. Malcolm Moran, "Players; Hamilton is Judging His Own Skating," *New York Times*, 26 January 1985.

28. Anugrah Kumar, "How Olympic Gold Medalist Scott Hamilton Found Jesus," *The Christian Post*, 28 January 2012. See: http:// www.christianpost.com/news/how-olympic-gold-medalist-scott-hamilton-found-jesus-68160/.

29. "I Am Second—Scott Hamilton," see: http://www.iamsecond.com/ seconds/scott-hamilton/.

30. Ibid.

31. Ibid.

32. Ibid.

ADOPTION MILESTONES: ADOPTION IN AMERICA

1. Source: The Adoption History Project (University of Oregon), February 24, 2012

CHAPTER THIRTEEN: FAITH HILL

1. CNN Larry King Live, "Interview with Faith Hill and Tim McGraw, 21 April 2006. See: http://www.cnn.com/ TRANSCRIPTS/0604/21/lkl.01.html

2. Jill Carlson, "My Town: Star to Stardom," Country Weekly, 12 July 2004. See: http://www.countryweekly.com/vault/my-town-star-stardom

3. "What I Know Now," People Magazine, 12 April 2004. See: http:// www.people.com/people/archive/article/0,,20149804,00.html

4. Ibid.

5. James L. Dickerson, *Faith Hill: A Piece of My Heart* (New York: St. Martin's Griffin, 2001), 9.

6. Ibid.

7. Ibid.

8. Ibid., 19.

9. Ibid., 17.
10. "Faith Hill: Five Fun Facts," *People Magazine*. See: http://www.people.com/people/faith_hill/
11. Dickerson, Ibid., 17.
12. Leah Ginsberg, "Faith Renewed," Good Housekeeping, 7 March 2007. See: http://www.goodhousekeeping.com/life/inspirational-stories/interviews/a15246/faith-hill-renewed-apr04/
13. Dickerson, Ibid., 23.
14. Ibid.
15. Ibid., 29.
16. "Celebrity Central: Faith Hill," *People Magazine*. See: http://www.people.com/people/faith_hill/biography/
17. Dickerson, Ibid., 30.
18. Ginsberg, "Faith Renewed," Ibid.
19. Ibid.
20. Ginsberg, Ibid.
21. Ibid.
22. Ibid.
23. Sarah Netemeyer, "Tim McGraw and Faith Hill: A True Love Story," Country Fancast, 17 February 2016. See: http://countryfancast.com/tim-mcgraw-faith-hill-love/
24. Dickerson, Ibid., 42.

CHAPTER FOURTEEN: JOHANN SEBASTIAN BACH

1. Martin Luther, "In the Very Midst of Life," 1524.
2. Christoph Wolff, *Johann Sebastian Bach: The Learned Musician* (New York: W.W. Norton, 2000), 18.
3. Ibid.
4. Ibid.
5. A. A. Milne (1882-1956).
6. "The Music of Johann Sebastian Bach," Christian Assemblies International. See: https://www.cai.org/bible-studies/music-johann-sebastian-bach.
7. Wolff, Ibid; see: https://www.nytimes.com/books/first/w/wolff-bach.html.

8. Sir Nicholas Kenyon, *The Faber Pocket Guide to Bach* (London: Faber and Faber, 2011), 73.
9. Wolff, Ibid., 33.
10. Ibid., 34.
11. Benjamin Disraeli (1804-1881).
12. "J.S. Bach: Soli Deo Gloria – To the Glory of God Alone," Church History Timeline. See: http://www.christianity.com/church/church-history/church-history-for-kids/j-s-bach-soli-deo-gloria-to-the-glory-of-god-alone-11635057.html.
13. "The Music of Johann Sebastian Bach," Ibid.
14. Carl Philipp Emmanuel Bach (1714-1788).

CHAPTER FIFTEEN: LEO TOLSTOY

1. Leo Tolstoy, *The Novels and Other Works of Lyof N. Tolstoi* (New York: Scribner's Sons, 1899-1902), 52.
2. Ibid.
3. Ibid., 104.
4. Ibid.
5. P. Biriukov, *Leo Tolstoy, His Life and Work: Autobiographical Memoirs, Letters amd Biographical Material* (New York: C. Scribner, 1906), 13.
6. Alexandra Tolstory, "Tolstoy and The Russian Peasant," *Russian Review*, April 1960. See: https://notesfromthestage.files.wordpress.com/2011/04/tolstoy-and-peasants1.pdf.
7. Biriukov, Ibid., 13.
8. Ibid., 35.
9. Ibid., 36.
10. Rosamund Bartlett, *Tolstoy: A Russian Life* (Boston, MA: Houghton Mifflin Harcourt , 2011), 36.
11. Aylmer Maude, *The Life of Tolstoy: First Fifty Years* (Oxford: Oxford University Press, 1987), 8.
12. Leo Tolstoy, Ibid., 50.
13. Ibid., 41.
14. Ibid.
15. Maude, Ibid., 6.
16. Tolstoy, Ibid., 59.

17. Henri Troyat, *Tolstoy* (Norwalk, CT: Easton Press, 1993), 28.
18. Tolstoy, Ibid., 63.
19. "Leo Tolstoy," *The Pittsburgh-Press*, 15 July 1906, 7.
20. Maude, Ibid., 53.
21. Leo Tolstoy, *Anna Karenina* (New York: Knopf, 1992), 1.
22. Leo Tolstoy, The Book Buyer: A Monthly Review of American and Foreign Literature, Charles Scribner's Sons, February 1905. See: https://books.google.com/books?id=x9wRAAAAYAAJ&pg=RA1-PA108&lpg=RA1-PA108&dq=%E2%80%9Clast+period+of+my+awakening+to+the+truth+which+has+given+me+the+highest+well-being+in+life+and+joyous+peace+in+view+of+approaching+death%22&source=bl&ots=ue3uMADYat&sig=2XsDWt3WAwzSlQ52R6Aj35JavkE&hl=en&sa=X&ved=0ahUKEwi4zLbJ6aPOAhUBzSYKHZyGDDgQ6AEIHDAA#v=onepage&q=%E2%80%9Clast%20period%20of%20my%20awakening%20to%20the%20truth%20which%20has%20given%20me%20the%20highest%20well-being%20in%20life%20and%20joyous%20peace%20in%20view%20of%20approaching%20death%22&f=false
23. Leo Tolstoy, *A Confession and Other Religious Writings* (New York: Viking Penguin, 1987).
24. Leo Tolstoy, *The Kingdom of God is Within You* (New York: T.Y. Crowell, 1899), 49.
25. Bartlett, Ibid., 414.

ADOPTION MILESTONES: EMBRYO ADOPTION

1. Interview with Marlene Strege, 2011.

CHAPTER SIXTEEN: THE ULTIMATE ADOPTION STORY: JESUS OF NAZARETH

1. Norman Vincent Peale, "When Christmas Comes," Marble Collegiate Church, 24 December 1982. See: http://www.marblechurch.org/connect/library/vincent-peale.
2. "H.G. Wells on the Historicity of Jesus," Apologetics 315. See: http://www.apologetics315.com/2013/06/hg-wells-on-historicity-of-jesus.html.
3. Phillips Brooks, "O Little Town of Bethlehem," 1867.

4. T.M. Moore, "Every Square Inch," Breakpoint, 12 December 2012. See: http://www.colsoncenter.org/the-center/columns/talking-points/18933-every-square-inch.

5. Jerry Bridges, *Holiness Day By Day: Transformational Thoughts For Your Spiritual Journey* (Colorado Springs, CO: NavPress, 2008).

6. John Polkinghorne, *Living With Hope: A Scientist Looks at Advent, Christmas and Epiphany* (Louisville, KY: Westminster John Knox Press, 2003), 79.

7. David Joseph Platt (1979–).